SECRET
BOSTON

A GUIDE TO THE WEIRD, WONDERFUL, AND OBSCURE

Kim Foley MacKinnon

Reedy Press
PO Box 5131
St. Louis, MO 63139
www.reedypress.com

Library of Congress Control Number: 2019952739
ISBN: 9781681062105

Design by Jill Halpin

Unless otherwise indicated, all photos are courtesy of the author or in the public domain.

Printed in the United States of America
20 21 22 23 24   5 4 3 2 1

DEDICATION

For Rob and Sadie, with all my love, and to all my friends who helped along the way.

CONTENTS

INTRODUCTION

So much of what we see on a daily basis we take for granted, especially in a place where we've grown up or lived for a long time. We often stop really seeing it. We pass right on by an unusual sculpture or a home with weird architecture without a second thought, but in this book, you'll learn the backstory to all sorts of things that are sometimes hidden in plain sight.

Here are a few of the questions I asked myself as I took a magnifying glass to the city around me and realized that there were plenty of places, despite writing about Boston for years, that I had no clue about: Did someone misplace a house from *Gone with the Wind* in Beacon Hill? Was the telephone really invented here? How did the Freedom Trail get established? What's the story with the furry-costumed musician playing around town? What's the deal with the mysterious round stone dated 1737 on the base of a building? Did someone build a house to spite his sibling? Did a molasses spill really kill twenty-one people? What's the deal with the painted lines on a bridge between Boston and Cambridge? How did a giant milk bottle come to be outside of the Boston Children's Museum? Why is there a twelve foot tall sculpture of a pear in Dorchester? Why is there a memorial dedicated to potatoes? And why is there a thirty-five-foot-tall statue of Mary perched atop the globe in East Boston?

Many people think they know everything there is to know about Boston. But when you dig a little deeper, there are so many layers, backstories, forgotten places, and unexplained art that it can be absolutely eye-opening. Flip open this book and be prepared to be surprised.

DRESSED UP DUCKS

Why are these duckling statues dressed in costumes?

It's not every day that you see bronze sculptures in a public space sporting football jerseys, Easter bonnets, or Santa Claus hats, but *Make Way for Ducklings* in the Boston Public Garden is no regular piece of public art.

Created by local sculptor Nancy Schön and based upon the beloved 1941 children's book of the same name by Robert McCloskey, Mrs. Mallard and her brood—Jack, Kack, Lack, Mack, Nack, Ouack, Pack, and Quack—have been a fixture in the park since 1987. In the book, the Mallard family has come to Boston to look for a home. They love the beautiful Public Garden and eventually make their way to an island in the Lagoon, where they make their home. The statues are a must-see stop for families and fans of the book.

What isn't in the book, and something that has certainly taken on a life of its own over the years, is the dressing up of the statues. If the Boston Bruins, New England Patriots, Boston Red Sox, or Boston Celtics make it to their respective finals, look for the ducks to be adorned in their sportswear. At Easter, they might have flowery bonnets atop their heads, and on St. Patrick's Day, they might be wearing jaunty green hats. Often, the costumes are courtesy of a sports team or a cultural institution, but sometimes an anonymous dresser makes a statement, such as when the ducks' heads were topped with pink hats during a major political protest, a very Boston thing to do.

After Raisa Gorbachev admired the Boston ducklings on a U.S. visit in 1990, Barbara Bush gave her a copy in 1991.

Look for costumes on the Make Way for Ducklings *statues in the Public Garden on holidays and big sporting events.*

MAKE WAY FOR DUCKLINGS SCULPTURE

WHAT A beloved sculpture from a children's book

WHERE Boston Public Garden, corner of Beacon and Charles Sts.

COST Free

PRO TIP If the weather is warm, head to the Lagoon to take a ride in a Swan Boat for a great family outing.

CAN'T BELIEVE YOUR EYES

Did someone misplace a house from *Gone with the Wind*?

Historic Beacon Hill, lined with cobblestoned streets, real gas streetlamps, and charming nineteenth-century townhouses, is classic, picture-perfect, postcard Boston. When you're walking down such a street, look down an alley, and spy a white, two-story, columned Greek Revival house, you're bound to do a doubletake.

Are you seeing things? Or did someone have odd taste in design, breaking the neighborhood norms? The answer is "sort of" to both questions.

The so-called Scarlett O'Hara House is a trompe l'oeil, an optical illusion that tricks your eye. While there is an actual shallow porch, the rest of the house is a facade. Details of its origin are sketchy, but it is said the "house" was created more than thirty years ago as an ingenious way to hide an unsightly concrete wall and/or protect people from walking off the ledge behind it. The facade's small porch leads to two separate homes on either side of the fake house.

Regardless, with the white wood siding, Ionic columns, and fake windows and shutters, it is a whimsical spot in a very staid neighborhood. Neighbors even decorate the front of the house during the holidays with a wreath, holly, and lights.

SCARLETT O'HARA HOUSE

WHAT An optical illusion

WHERE Rollins Pl.

COST Free

PRO TIP The alley is private property, so stick to the street.

The facade's small porch leads into two separate homes on either side of it. One of the homes sold for $1.4 million in 2018.

Located at the end of a Beacon Hill alley, this house plays tricks on your eyes.

DEATH NOTICE

Is this revered library haunted?

It is home to the largest collection in the world of books from George Washington's library. Ralph Waldo Emerson and Louisa May Alcott are just two of its most famous visitors and members over the years. There are portraits by John Singer Sargent and pastels by John Singleton Copley on its walls.

If this were a guessing game, you might name the Boston Public Library or the Museum of Fine Arts, Boston as the repository of such items, but you'd be wrong. The Boston Athenæum, founded in 1807, predates them both by decades. Today, the library has more than half a million volumes, along with its artwork and other collections.

As such a historic part of Boston's past, the Athenæum naturally has many stories of its own to tell, one of which involves Nathaniel Hawthorne and a ghost. One of its lifetime members, Reverend Thaddeus Mason Harris (1768–1842), was a frequent visitor to the library, supposedly even after his death.

According to the folklore surrounding the Athenæum, Hawthorne told the story of seeing Reverend Harris in the library in 1842—reading his own obituary in the morning paper. The author spotted the reverend at the Athenæum frequently in the weeks following the first sighting. Many

years later, a friend in England insisted that Hawthorne record the tale. It was published in the popular literary weekly Littell's *The Living Age* in 1900.

Certainly, the phrase "If these walls could talk" was made for places like this library!

Look for the portrait of Hannah Adams (1755–1831) on the first floor of the library. She is said to be the first professional American female writer and was also the very first person to have a monument in Mount Auburn Cemetery.

TAKE A DEEP BREATH

Why is there a museum at Mass General Hospital?

Boston is a city of firsts, from the first subway to the first free public library, so it should come as no surprise that the city was the home to the first public demonstration of surgical anesthesia.

ETHER DOME

WHAT First time anesthesia was administered in public

WHERE Massachusetts General Hospital, 55 Fruit St., Bulfinch Bldg., 4th Floor

COST Free

PRO TIP The dome is generally open Monday through Friday from 9 a.m. to 5 p.m., unless there's a meeting, so call ahead.

Sure, it would be unheard of these days to go under the knife without, well, going under, but that wasn't always the case. We take anesthesia for granted now, but until the mid-1800s, surgery was usually an excruciatingly painful experience. On October 16, 1846, Dr. William T. G. Morton and Dr. John Collins Warren changed that forever in a public demonstration. Morton administered ether anesthetic to patient Gilbert Abbott just before Warren removed a tumor from the patient's neck. It was reported that Abbott slept during the operation and afterwards said that he had felt no pain.

The historic event took place in a surgical amphitheater, today known as the Ether Dome, which now serves as a small museum as well as an occasional classroom. Back in its heyday, though,

Besides the landmark surgery, Mass General is the site of many other breakthroughs, such as identifying appendicitis (1886), performing the first reattachment of a severed limb (1962), and developing the first laser treatment to remove tattoos (1988).

This surgical amphitheater, known today as the Ether Dome, was the site of the first surgery where ether was ever used.

A unique painting of this medical breakthrough hangs in the Ether Dome.

between 1821 and 1868, more than eight thousand operations were performed there. There is a small collection of artifacts, including early medical tools and an Egyptian mummy, but the main attraction is *Ether Day, 1846*, a painting with a cool story all its own.

At the time, the surgery was recorded in photographs and paintings, leaving a clear visual record for us today. In 2000 several Mass General doctors decided to commission a painting of the scene and donate it to the hospital. The artists, who wanted the work to be as realistic as possible, used Mass General physicians to stage the surgery, in authentic clothing and accessories, including replicas of pocket watches, monocles, and frock coats. They even applied fake mustaches and used fake blood in the re-creation. A year later, the six-by-eight-foot mural was unveiled.

PHONE HOME

Where did the first transmittance of sound over wires occur?

A small, easy-to-miss granite block tucked against a low wall on the plaza in front of the John F. Kennedy Building on Cambridge Street is a rather modest marker for a quite momentous event, one that would change the world.

This spot, as a plaque on the top of the marker states, is the "Birthplace of the Telephone. Here, on June 2, 1875, Alexander Graham Bell and Thomas A. Watson first transmitted sound over wires. This successful experiment was completed in a fifth floor garret at what was then 109 Court Street and marked the beginning of world-wide telephone service." On the front, there is a depiction of the invention.

In March 1876, three days after his telephone patent was issued, Bell made his iconic demand to Watson over the first telephone: "Mr. Watson, come here, I want to see you." With that statement, transmitted over the wires into the next room, the pathway to the cell phone was forged.

Almost one year after that, on February 12, 1877, Bell made a call from a lecture hall in Salem, Massachusetts, to *The Boston Globe*'s newspaper offices miles away in Boston, once again making history. "SENT BY TELEPHONE: The First Newspaper Dispatch Sent by a Human Voice Over the Wires," read *The Globe*'s headline the next day, marking the first time a journalist filed an article over the telephone.

Alexander Graham Bell was a professor of the mechanism of speech in Boston University's School of Oratory from 1874 to 1879.

Look for a small block marking a momentous event, where Alexander Graham Bell and Thomas A. Watson first transmitted sound over wires.

BIRTHPLACE OF THE TELEPHONE MARKER

WHAT Where the first phone call occurred

WHERE Cambridge St.

COST Free

PRO TIP Did you know the word "decibel" was derived from Bell's name? It is a unit of sound.

A HEAD CASE, AMONG OTHER THINGS

Where can you learn about fascinating medical case studies?

The Warren Anatomical Museum grew from the collection donated by Harvard anatomist and surgeon John Collins Warren in 1847. It's one of the last surviving anatomy and pathology museum collections in the United States. Warren had amassed a large private collection of human and animal specimens, prepared by him and purchased in the United States or abroad, which he had used for teaching. When he retired, he donated it to the university. Over the years, others donated items of interest.

One of the most well-known is that of the skull, life cast, and tamping iron of Phineas Gage, one of neurology's most famous cases. Gage, a railroad worker, sustained a traumatic brain injury in 1848 when a 3' 7" inch iron rod went through his head.

The accident cost Gage an eye and altered his personality, but he survived. His changes helped doctors begin to understand the localized nature of personality and identity.

Other notable items at the museum include the phrenological collection of Johann Gaspar Spurzheim (1776-1832), including a cast of his own skull. Spurzheim was famous for his contributions to phrenology, a field of neuroscience focused on studying the shapes of the skulls in relation to the activity levels of certain functional areas of the brain.

The museum is being redesigned as part of the larger Countway Library renovation. The anticipated reopening is spring 2021.

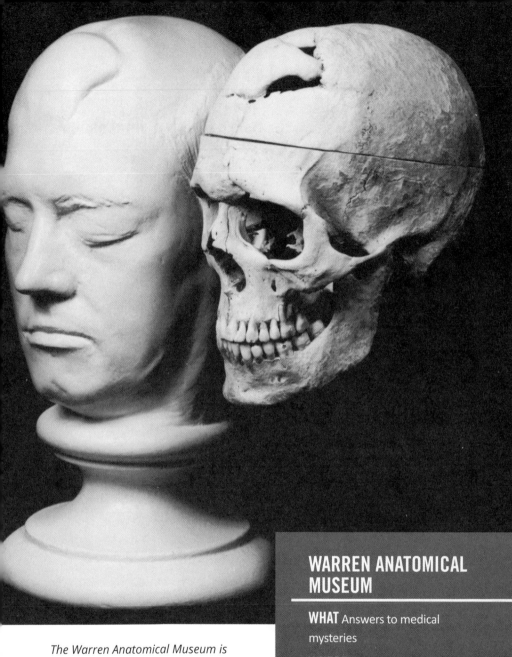

The Warren Anatomical Museum is home to all sorts of medical curiosities, including the skull, life cast, and tamping iron of Phineas Gage, one of neurology's most famous cases. Photo courtesy of the Warren Anatomical Museum.

WARREN ANATOMICAL MUSEUM

WHAT Answers to medical mysteries

WHERE 10 Shattuck St.

COST Free

PRO TIP You can see the collection online too.

MOVIE MAGIC

Where can you sit on the bench from a pivotal movie scene in *Good Will Hunting*?

Boston has been used as the setting for countless television shows and movies, from *Cheers* and *Boston Legal* to *The Departed*, but one of the most beloved is *Good Will Hunting*, released in 1997.

The breakout movie for writers and actors Matt Damon and Ben Affleck tells the story of Will Hunting (Matt Damon), a janitor at MIT who happens to be a genius but isn't living up to his potential. Robin Williams plays a psychologist who helps him to see that he can do much more with his life, but it takes a while to get him there.

Damon and Affleck, both Boston natives, took great care in shooting the movie and made the city as important a character as any of the actors. One favorite location from the movie that fans love to visit is the L Street Tavern in South Boston, where Will and his best friend, Chuckie Sullivan (played by Affleck), hung out.

But perhaps the most vital scene of the film takes place in the Boston Public Garden, where Williams's character basically reads Will the riot act as they sit on a bench near the Lagoon. It's a powerful and moving scene, which ends with the now-famous quote, "Your move, chief."

After Robin Williams died in 2014, fans turned the bench into a makeshift memorial, leaving flowers and writing quotes from the film on the ground in chalk.

GOOD WILL HUNTING BENCH

WHAT Famous bench from movie

WHERE Boston Public Garden

COST Free

PRO TIP Head over to 84 Beacon Street to see the facade of the bar from the television show *Cheers*.

Take a seat where Robin Williams and Matt Damon had a heart-to-heart in the film Good Will Hunting.

To find the bench, enter the Public Garden from Arlington Street and follow the lakeside path north from the western end of the bridge. It's the third one.

TRAILBLAZERS

Are there other trails to follow in Boston besides the Freedom Trail?

The Freedom Trail is an iconic attraction in Boston, a magnet for millions of visitors and a familiar sight to those who live in the city, but it's not the only historic game in town. The Black Heritage Trail, a one-and-a-half-mile walk, leads to fourteen historic sites and details the lives of the free black community of Beacon Hill from the late eighteenth century through the nineteenth century. While the North End and the West End were home to some black Bostonians, most of the two thousand African Americans in the city lived in the shadow of the Massachusetts State House on Beacon Hill, just below the homes of Boston's most prominent white citizens.

The trail leads to former homes, schools, businesses, and churches, as well as several stations on the Underground Railroad. Highlights include the *54th Regiment Memorial*, which commemorates the first black regiment recruited in the North during the Civil War; the Phillips School, one of Boston's first integrated educational institutions; and the African Meeting House, which was built by free black laborers in 1806 and is considered the oldest surviving church building for African Americans in the United States.

One notable Underground Railroad station is the John J. Smith House. Smith, who moved to Boston in the late 1840s, operated a barbershop that soon became a focal point for abolitionist meetings and a way station for escaped slaves.

The National Park Service leads free ninety-minute tours seasonally.

Follow the 1.5-mile Black Heritage Trail to 14 historic sites detailing the lives of the free black community of Beacon Hill from the late 18th century through the 19th century. Photo courtest of Kyle Klein.

Another important station is the Lewis and Harriet Hayden House. The Haydens escaped from slavery in Kentucky and moved to Boston, where Lewis Hayden became a prominent abolitionist. The story goes that the Haydens threatened to ignite the kegs of gunpowder they stored in their home if slave catchers entered the premises.

BLACK HERITAGE TRAIL

WHAT Fourteen historic sites

WHERE Beacon Hill

COST Free (though some sites charge admission to enter)

PRO TIP A Black Heritage Trail on Nantucket Island features nine stops and is divided into two segments, Downtown and New Guinea. New Guinea is the section of Nantucket where blacks lived in the eighteenth and nineteenth centuries.

WEATHER REPORT

What do the lights on the Old John Hancock Building mean?

One of the first things I learned when I moved to Boston eons ago was that if I wanted to know the weather report, I just had to look to the John Hancock Building, which is located at 200 Berkeley Street in the Back Bay.

Now called the Berkeley Building, the formerly-known-as-the-John Hancock Building was built in 1947 and at the time was the second-tallest building in the city at 495 feet. It was built for the John Hancock Insurance Company. It is not to be confused with the John Hancock Tower, built in 1967, which is now named 200 Clarendon (its address), but most locals still call it the Hancock Tower, a common Bostonian practice. But I digress.

The weather beacon was installed on the Old Hancock Building in 1950 and inspired the following poem, which, while commonly known to locals, is not attributed to anyone I could find.

Solid blue, clear view
Flashing blue, clouds due
Solid red, rain ahead
Flashing red, snow instead.

Don't confuse the glass-sided "new" John Hancock Building with the former one.

Besides telling the weather, this building gives fans a head's up when Red Sox games are cancelled.

BERKELEY BUILDING

WHAT A weather beacon on a building

WHERE 200 Berkeley St.

COST Free

PRO TIP During baseball season, flashing red means the Red Sox game is cancelled due to bad weather.

TEA TIME

What's the meaning of the decorative bronze doors on Stuart Street?

Something might seem slightly out of place as you stroll down Stuart Street, where office buildings line the street and busy pedestrians rush about. Two elaborately designed twelve-foot bronze doors stand out for their uniqueness.

The building is owned by Liberty Mutual, but the doors were created for the Salada Tea Company's headquarters in 1927. Owner and founder Peter C. Larkin commissioned the doors to tell the story of the company, which was founded in 1892 in Toronto. In 1917 Larkin moved the company to Boston into a building designed especially for his company by architects Edward Dana Densmore and Gifford LeClear. The Salada Tea Company was famous for being the first company to sell tea that was packaged in foil, which eventually led to creation of the modern tea bag.

Sculptor Henry Wilson designed the doors to show ten scenes from Ceylon tea plantations. In them the tea is harvested, sorted, and dried, then carried to the ships by elephant or by the workers, who balance boxes of tea on their heads. Even the marble outer doorframe is a stunner—carved by artist Caesar Caira, it offers a more classical take, with a statue of the Greek goddess Demeter on top and elephants on the sides. In 1927 the doors won the coveted silver medal at the Paris Salon.

Henry Wilson's only other work in the United States was the bronze doors at the Cathedral of Saint John the Divine in New York. Most of his works are located in England.

The 12-foot ornate doors on Stuart Street once marked the entrance to the Salada Tea Company. Photo by Rob MacKinnon.

SALADA TEA DOORS

WHAT Former fancy company entrance

WHERE 330 Stuart St.

COST Free

PRO TIP Salada is still produced, though it is owned by the Harris Tea Company.

TIME CAPSULES

Where can you see museum-quality dioramas in an office lobby?

Newbury Street is a shopping and dining hotspot, with visitors and locals alike flocking to the popular Back Bay street for everything from cosmos to high-priced kicks, but it does have other attractions. One such spot is located in an unlikely place, in the lobby of a gray granite building called The Newbry, located on Newbury between Berkeley and Clarendon Streets.

Unless you had some specific business in the building, there's no reason you'd go in. Why would you? But inside the lobby, there are four inset windows with intricate dioramas, each showing a tiny scene of Boston spanning thousands of years. The dioramas were commissioned by the Boston Society of Natural History in 1863 and created by Sarah Ann Rockwell.

While excavating the Boylston Street subway in 1915, workers found wooden posts driven into the ground. Researchers determined that the wood dated back to 2500 B.C. when the native Americans built traps in the mud flats of the Back Bay to catch fish.

Another diorama is of the William Blaxton/Blackstone House. After he graduated Cambridge, Blaxton came as an Anglican clergyman to the Shawmut Peninsula with other colonists in 1623—seven years before the Puritans. He

---

The Boston Society of Natural History was founded in 1830. It displayed its collections in temporary facilities until 1864, when it opened as the New England Museum of Natural History in the Back Bay. That museum is now known as the Museum of Science, Boston.

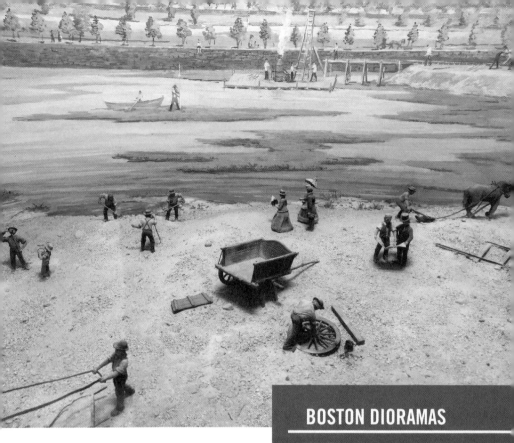

One of four intricate dioramas in an office lobby is called the "Filling of the Back Bay (1858)," which depicts the beginning stages of that long project.

BOSTON DIORAMAS

WHAT Tiny scenes of Boston

WHERE 501 Boylston St.

COST Free

PRO TIP Technically on Boylston Street, the public entrance is on Newbury Street.

remained by himself after they went home and built a house on the future Boston Common, becoming the first of the intrepid men of Boston.

Moving up to the 1800s, the next diorama is called the *Filling of the Back Bay* (1858), which shows the beginning stages of that long construction project. And finally, the last scene is the Building the *Boston Society of Natural History* (1863), an intricate scene which shows how sparse the area once was.

WRITER'S BLOCKS

Did the Freedom Trail really get established through a newspaper column?

Anyone who's ever been to Boston, or even read about it, has surely heard about the Freedom Trail. It's the city's most famous attraction, linking sixteen historic sites along an easy-to-follow red line (sometimes painted and sometimes made of brick). But have you ever wondered how it came about? It didn't spring out of nowhere, after all.

Improbably enough, it came from Bill Schofield, an editor and columnist for the old Herald-Traveler newspaper. In 1951 Schofield realized that it was difficult to navigate among the various revolutionary historic sites around the city. He enlisted Bob Winn, sexton of the North End's Old North Church at the time, to help, and the pair came up with a draft of a walking path. Then Schofield laid out his idea in a column.

On March 8, 1951, he wrote, "All I'm suggesting is that we mark out a 'Puritan Path' or 'Liberty Loop' or 'Freedom's Way' or whatever you want to call it, so [visitors and locals will] know where to start and what course to follow . . . [Y]ou could do the trick on a budget of just a few dollars and a bucket of paint."

A few weeks later, his column read, "A telephone call from Mayor John B. Hynes brings the news that the city intends to go along with the Freedom Way plan proposed here." In short order, signs were put up to mark an approximately one-mile-long route from Boston Common to the North End, but it took a while for the red path to be realized. Finally, in 1958, the red line was added, and over the years the route changed to include

FOUNDING OF THE FREEDOM TRAIL

WHAT Origin story

WHERE Boston

COST Free

PRO TIP You can pick up a free map at the Boston Common Visitor Information Center.

The story of how the Freedom Trail was created might come as a surprise to many.

Charlestown and more sites. Today, it's two and a half miles long, and most people would find it difficult to imagine the city without it.

Other trails, such as the Black Heritage Trail and the Women's Heritage Trail, have been added over the years to help people find more of the city's important historical sites.

RETURN APPEARANCE

Why is there a statue of Edgar Allan Poe in Boston?

Edgar Allan Poe's feelings about Boston, or at least the writers of his time, are pretty clear.

From a letter Poe wrote to a friend in 1849:

"I wish you would come down on the Frogpondians. They are getting worse and worse, and pretend not to be aware that there are any literary people out of Boston. The worst and most disgusting part of the matter is, that the Bostonians are really, as a race, far inferior in point of anything beyond mere talent, to any other set upon the continent of N. A."

Despite those sentiments, Boston still loves Poe, who was born here on January 19, 1809. When he was a young child, both his parents died and he went to live with tobacco merchant John Allan and his wife, Frances Valentine Allan, in Richmond, Virginia. Poe's life was never particularly easy, and his relationship with the Boston literati was never good.

But no matter. The Edgar Allen Poe Foundation of Boston felt a statue was needed to commemorate the poet. They raised the money to fund it and convinced the city to install it, which it finally did in October of 2014.

Artist Stefanie Rocknak designed the life-sized bronze-based statue, called *Poe Returning to Boston*, which depicts Poe striding vigorously through the city, jacket flowing, case in hand, with papers flying out behind him. A giant raven leads the way, while

---

Following the successful achievement of its primary objective, installation of the statue, the Poe Foundation of Boston filed for dissolution in December 2014 and formally dissolved in 2015.

While Edgar Allen Poe was never a fan of Boston, he was born here. This statue pays tribute the author.

a heart, reminiscent of the one that beats ominously throughout Poe's short story "The Tell-Tale Heart," sits on a pile of books behind him. The statue is as dramatic as some of Poe's works.

POE RETURNING TO BOSTON

WHAT Edgar Allen Poe statue

WHERE Corner of Boylston and Charles Sts.

COST Free

PRO TIP Poe faces away from the Frog Pond, a pointed reference to his "Frogpondian" feelings.

TABLE TALK

What hotel has hosted generations of Boston's movers and shakers, including the famous Saturday Club of literary greats?

The Omni Parker House, founded by Harvey D. Parker in 1855, is one of Boston's most famous hotels and the country's longest continuously operating hotel. Over the years, everyone who is anyone has made an appearance there.

Politicians, including Ulysses S. Grant, Franklin Delano Roosevelt, John F. Kennedy Jr., Thomas "Tip" O'Neill, and Bill Clinton, have stayed, spoken, or dined there. Sports figures, such as Babe Ruth, Ted Williams, and David Ortiz, have frequented the hotel. A long list of visiting performers includes names like Sarah Bernhardt, Edwin Booth, Joan Crawford, Judy Garland, James Dean, Yo-Yo Ma, and Ben Affleck.

But, perhaps most famously, the hotel was home to the legendary nineteenth-century Saturday Club, where writers of the day met for socializing. Started informally by Ralph Waldo Emerson, Horatio Woodman, and Samuel Gray Ward, the club was also home to Louis Agassiz, Richard Henry Dana Jr., Henry Wadsworth Longfellow, James Russell Lowell, and Oliver Wendell Holmes.

Traditionally, the club met at 3 p.m. on the last Saturday of every month for meals and conversation. It incorporated in 1886, for the purpose of "having conversation and discussion upon historical, literary, scientific, and artistic subjects." The

The famous Parker House roll and the Boston cream pie (the Official State Dessert of Massachusetts) were invented at the hotel.

The Omni Parker House was host to any number of famous faces. Photo courtesy of the hotel.

group met at the Parker House until 1902, when it moved to the Union Club.

Today, you can have a drink at the hotel while sitting under silhouettes of some of these famous faces in Parker's Bar.

HOME OF THE SATURDAY CLUB

WHAT Where literary greats met

WHERE 60 School St.

COST Free

PRO TIP A lot of famous faces have also worked at the hotel over the years, including Emeril Lagasse, Malcolm X, and Ho Chi Minh.

TUNEFUL TEDDY

What's the story with the furry-costumed musician playing around town?

Don't be alarmed if you see a giant bear playing a keytar in the subway or on the street. It's just another regular day in the neighborhood and you just spotted Keytar Bear. This busker, who is either delightful or creepy, depending upon your perspective, has been performing on the streets for the last five years or so.

Somehow able to maintain his anonymity despite several media interviews and attempts to unmask him, the musician delights in being mysterious. He mostly plays popular dance music, like Prince and Michael Jackson, on his electronic keyboard/guitar hybrid, which is hooked up to an amplifier. While you never know when and where he might pop up, he does like to frequent the subway, Faneuil Hall, and Boston Common.

Over the years, Keytar has been the target of several violent attacks, but he keeps coming back to delight his dedicated fans, who aren't just random passersby. Keytar has played in clubs, for the city, and at festivals. A local beer company, Trillium Brewing, even named a beer after him, the Keytar Bear Double IPA. Make sure you keep your eyes peeled as you walk around Boston!

There's no way of predicting where Keytar will be playing, so just keep your eyes peeled.

Look for this fuzzy busker in public spaces in the city.

KEYTAR BEAR

WHAT An unusual busker

WHERE Anywhere, any time!

COST Free, but it's friendly to tip!

PRO TIP Keytar won't talk, so don't bother trying.

HIT THE HIGHWAY

Why is there a steel beam sticking out the sidewalk?

One of Boston's stranger memorials is a tribute to a lost highway, specifically the elevated part of the John F. Fitzgerald Expressway (often called the Southeast Expressway), a highway most Bostonians would prefer to forget.

Located on a corner near Quincy Market is a lone beam painted green. Anyone would be forgiven for walking right on by, but if you stop to read the plaque mounted on it, you'd learn that it's the last remaining piece of the reviled expressway that's left. The plaque reads in part:

"This structural column, known as Bent 38, still rests on its original foundations and is the only piece of the elevated highway that was left undisturbed by construction. It remains as a memorial to the Expressway and to the impact that the health of our transportation systems have upon the life of our community. It also symbolizes the labor of scores of men and women who work to improve our infrastructure every day."

During the 1950s, when it was built, the elevated John F. Fitzgerald Expressway was both ambitious and controversial. More than twenty thousand people were displaced from their homes, hundreds of buildings were demolished, and it cut off the North End and the waterfront from the city. For all the hopes that it would relieve traffic, it didn't.

The Ted Williams Tunnel in East Boston, between the land-based approach and the underwater section, is ninety feet below the surface of Boston Harbor, the deepest such connection in North America.

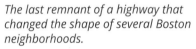

The last remnant of a highway that changed the shape of several Boston neighborhoods.

The Expressway's daily capacity grew from approximately seventy-five thousand vehicles in 1959 to nearly two hundred thousand vehicles in 1990. Pollution and traffic jams became the norm. Finally, the city embarked on another massive fix. From 1990 to 2007, the Central Artery/Tunnel Project, aka the "Big Dig," redirected I-93 into a network of downtown tunnels and created the Rose Kennedy Greenway and other parks.

BENT 38

WHAT Last remnant

WHERE On the corner of Clinton St. and John F. Fitzgerald Surface Rd.

COST Free

PRO TIP In total, the project built 161 lane miles of highway, about half in tunnels, and four major highway interchanges in a seven-and-a-half-mile corridor.

NAME GAME

Why is Boston called the "Hub of the Universe"?

Boston has several nicknames: Beantown, City on a Hill, Athens of America, and of course, the grandiose Hub of the Universe.

Oliver Wendell Holmes used the words "hub of the solar system" in a series of essays about Boston called *The Autocrat at the Breakfast Table* that were published in *The Atlantic Monthly* in 1858.

It wasn't meant as a compliment.

To wit: "Boston State-House is the hub of the solar system. You couldn't pry that out of a Boston man, if you had the tire of all creation straightened out for a crowbar."

Clearly, Holmes was poking fun at Boston's perceived self-importance, but like many pejoratives, it got flipped to be a badge of honor. Eventually the Hub of the Solar System turned into the Hub of the Universe, and these days, the city is often referred to simply as the Hub.

While all of this is well documented in historic materials, there is also a fun marker pairing the nickname with a long-gone beloved Boston institution, Filene's Basement, a discount

Holmes is also credited with coining the term "Boston Brahmin," a nickname for the wealthy enlightened class of Boston's mid-nineteenth century, also in *The Atlantic Monthly*.

This marker celebrates a long-gone beloved shop and celebrates Boston's place as the Hub of the Universe.

department store. The Basement had a date-based system of automatically marking down the clothes it got from upscale Filene's (its mothership located above). It went bust in 2007, but its name lives on. Look for the large marker with its name and the words "Hub of the Universe" embedded in front of the old Filene's (now a Primark) on Washington Street.

NOT SO SECRET

Can you really visit a masonic lodge without being a member?

The masons are generally seen as a secretive sort, with lots of rituals, handshakes, and a membership limited only to men. On their website, they describe their organization as "the world's oldest and largest Fraternity. It aims to promote Friendship, Morality, and Brotherly Love among its members."

But just because it's a membership-only organization doesn't mean that the members don't welcome curious people. The Grand Lodge of Masons in Massachusetts, built in 1898, opens its doors to the public for tours. The building is quite beautiful, with six meeting halls, a research library dedicated to Freemasonry, and the administrative offices. It's the oldest lodge in the Western Hemisphere and the third oldest in the world.

On a tour, visitors will get to see the headstone of Henry Price, the founder of Freemasonry in the United States; the Corinthian Hall, which features unique architectural designs and portraits of George Washington, Benjamin Franklin, Joseph Warren, and the Marquis de Lafayette (all original Freemasons); and other treasures that symbolize Masonic themes. The tall ceilings and mosaics floors are stunning, with an attention to detail that is impressive.

Freemasonry was a big deal in Colonial America. Besides Washington, Franklin, Warren, and Lafayette, other masons include Paul Revere, John Hancock, John Sullivan, Baron

---

The current building at 186 Tremont Street is the third Grand Lodge structure erected on the site.

The Grand Lodge of Masons is a gorgeous building and public tours are offered to explore the interior.

GRAND LODGE

WHAT Mason headquarters

WHERE 186 Tremont St.

COST Free

PRO TIP Public tours are available Monday through Friday on the hour between 10 a.m. and 2 p.m. On Saturdays, tours are on the half hour from 10 a.m. to 1:30 p.m.

Friedrich von Steuben, Nathanael Greene, and John Paul Jones. You can learn more on one of the fascinating tours (women welcome too!).

LOVE AT FIRST SIGHT

Where is there a statue that Democrats think is for them but really is for children?

Located just outside the entrance to Old City Hall stands a life-size statue of a donkey. Passersby would likely think that Democratic lawmakers had the statue installed as a tribute to their party. They'd be wrong. The statue's story is much more adorable than that.

Roger Webb, founder of the Architectural Heritage Foundation and Preservation Massachusetts, was visiting Italy in the mid-1990s when he happened upon the statue.

Below are excerpts from a letter written by Webb to the Boston Preservation Alliance in 2015, which explains the whole story in his own words:

"Traveling in Italy I fell in love with a donkey. Almost every Italian city has outdoor statues—historical, religious and sometimes beloved animals. These statues receive pats of affection from persons passing by and this leaves on the statue a shiny-reflective surface, evidence of their continuing strokes of connection.

"Florence of all Italian cities perhaps has the most outdoor statuary and is blessed with several ateliers that produce these statues in all sizes and shapes. I happened upon one of these shops in Florence years ago and wandered through their collections. My eye fell upon a life-size donkey hidden behind a large statue of a hog and Michelangelo's *David* with a saintly woman kneeling in prayer. The donkey looked at me and we

To appease Republicans, a set of bronze footprints was installed in front of the donkey, with an inscribed elephant and the words "Stand in Opposition."

This little donkey wasn't actually purchased for the Democratic Party.

fell in love. I pictured this little donkey in Boston on the Freedom Trail—perhaps in front of Old City Hall. I have always wanted a statue that would be particularly pleasing to children."

Webb shipped it home and presented his idea to the city, which flat-out refused to take it, saying it didn't belong. When he came up with a story of how the donkey could represent the Democratic Party, since Boston's politics had been dominated for over a century by Democratic mayors, the city was won over and the donkey was installed in 1998.

TRENDSETTER

How did saving a historic building set a trend toward preservation and reuse?

Roger Webb knew right where to put the donkey (see previous entry) because he was instrumental in saving Old City Hall from demolition thirty years earlier. In 1966 he founded the nonprofit Architectural Heritage Foundation, which negotiated a ninety-nine-year lease on the building and turned it into offices and a restaurant.

In the 1960s a new City Hall was built in Government Center, and the fate of the "Old" City Hall building, where for 104 years thirty-eight mayors conducted official business, was uncertain. Webb had a radical idea to turn the government building into a privately held enterprise in which commercial businesses could rent space—a practice that was definitely not the norm at the time. His vision saved the building and launched a movement to preserve other historic buildings instead of tearing them down.

It's not just the building that's historic; the very ground it sits on was the original location of Boston Latin School, America's first public school. Built in 1635, the school educated such illustrious attendees as Benjamin Franklin, John Hancock, and Samuel Adams. There is a mosaic marking the school's location, as well as a statue of Ben Franklin, which was installed in 1856 and was the first portrait statue to be erected in the city.

The building, constructed in 1865, was actually the third City Hall to be built in this spot.

The saving of Old City Hall marked a turning point in architecture to reuse historic buildings instead of destroying them.

OLD CITY HALL

WHAT Historic grounds

WHERE 45 School St.

COST Free

PRO TIP The Ruth's Chris Steak House is one of the businesses located in the building.

HOT POT

What's the deal with the steaming kettle hanging over Starbucks?

Not every landmark and eye-catching object you see in Boston is imbued with importance. Items you spot may be old, even historic, but that doesn't mean they have meaning beyond what they represent. Sometime a cigar is just a cigar.

One of the more novel examples of advertising around town is the giant steaming tea kettle, which, somewhat ironically, hangs over a Starbucks today. The kettle, which really does produce puffs of steam, was created in the 1870s to advertise the Oriental Tea Company in Boston's old Scollay Square. At a time when not everyone could read, a giant tea pot to advertise a tea company made perfect sense.

Its fame grew exponentially when the company held a public contest on New Year's Day in 1875 to guess how much tea the kettle could hold. The event, which the *Boston Globe* estimated drew eight thousand to twelve thousand spectators, kicked off in a hilarious fashion, "putting no less than eight small boys and a tall man inside the kettle, which contained this small society with ease." After they got out, water was added, measuring a total of 227 gallons, 2 quarts, 1 pint, and 3 gills. The contest drew more than thirteen thousand guesses, which resulted in eight winners. Each one received about five pounds of tea as their prize.

The kettle spent many years outside the Oriental Tea Company. Over the years, it moved from one location to

A gill (pronounced "*jill*") is an antiquated form of liquid measurement, the equivalent of one-half cup in today's measures.

Since the 1870s, this teakettle has served as an enticing advertisement.

GIANT TEA KETTLE

WHAT Ad for the ages

WHERE 63 Court St.

COST Free

PRO TIP It's easier to see the steam from the kettle on a cloudy day.

another as buildings were torn down, finally ending up at its current location on Court Street. While the Oriental Tea Company is long gone, its advertising stroke of genius lives on, as does the practice of crazy stunts to grab the public's attention and get what's in their wallets.

ROCK ON

What's the deal with the round stone at the base of a building?

In a city bursting with history and landmarks, it's almost bizarre that no one knows the real story behind the two-foot round granite stone embedded in the side of a building near Faneuil Hall. There's a carved inscription below the stone simply stating, "Boston Stone 1737."

Why is the stone there? Who placed it there? What's the significance of the 1737 date? Theories abound, but there is no definitive or authoritative source. Some say Thomas Childs brought the stone from England in 1700. Childs owned a paint mill at that location and may have used the stone to grind his pigments.

Another story claims—incorrectly—that the stone sits at the geographic center of Boston and that surveyors used it as the measuring point for distances to places around the city, much as the Romans were said to use the London Stone.

Yet others say that a shopkeeper on Marshall Street may have created the legend around the stone as a way to drum up business in the area. Since it still serves as a magnet for foot traffic to this day, maybe that's the most likely explanation!

The building above the Boston Stone is the Boston Stone Gift Shop. You can pick up souvenirs after getting a photo of the stone.

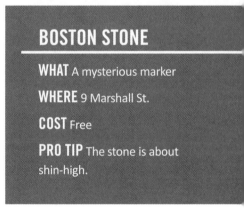

No one knows how or why this round stone exists or what the date under it means.

BOSTON STONE

WHAT A mysterious marker

WHERE 9 Marshall St.

COST Free

PRO TIP The stone is about shin-high.

BOTTOMS UP

Was the Ward Eight cocktail invented in Boston?

Maybe there's something in the nature of drinking alcohol that leads to a variety of cocktail origin stories, but while the provenance of many classic drinks is murky, the Ward Eight story seems to truly belong to Boston.

WARD 8

WHAT Classic cocktail

WHERE Yvonne's (2 Winter Pl.) and bars everywhere

COST Varies

PRO TIP The speakeasy-style restaurant is hidden behind the facade of a hair salon.

The long-shuttered Locke-Ober restaurant, an institution in the city from its opening in 1875, was a favorite with the powerful men of Boston (women couldn't even eat in the main dining room until the 1970s!), in particular, politicians.

As the story goes, in 1898 Martin Lomasney won a seat for the Massachusetts General Court from Ward Eight, and he and his cronies went to their favorite bar to celebrate. The Locke-Ober's bartender, Tom Hussion, was tasked with creating a drink to toast his victory, and thus the Ward Eight was born. Ironically, Lomasney was a prohibitionist! In 2012 the famous spot permanently closed. In 2015 the chic restaurant Yvonne's took its place, but the Ward Eight is still on the menu!

Yvonne's makes its Ward Eight with rye, sherry, grenadine, lemon, and orange.

The Ward Eight cocktail, allegedly invented in Boston, can still be had at Yvonne's. Photo by Nina Gallant.

The original recipe, according to *Mr. Boston: Official Bartender's Guide*, is as follows:
- 2 ounces rye whiskey
- ¾ ounce fresh lemon juice
- ½ ounce simple syrup
- ½ ounce grenadine
- Orange and lemon half-wheels
- Maraschino cherry

Shake with ice and strain into a red-wine glass filled with ice. Garnish with the orange, lemon, and cherry.

LOST TO TIME

How did this alley get its name?

One of Boston's oldest alleys has a curious name, but no one seems to have the definitive story on how Pi Alley was named. The downtown pedestrian walkway is a convenient shortcut from Washington Street to Old City Hall. A marker on the ground simply reads Pi Alley, but there's no explanation posted anywhere.

On the website of the Pi Alley Garage (located adjacent to the alley), there's a brief description and a link to a *Boston Globe* article speculating on its origins. Two theories have been presented. The first is that the alley was named for shops that used to be set up to serve local workers, and a popular dish was meat pie, hence the alley's name (although spelled wrong).

The more plausible explanation is that back in the day when Washington Street was home to most of the printing presses for the city's newspapers, including the *Boston Herald*, the *Boston Post*, and the *Boston Globe*, printers and typesetters would visit bars in the alley. They'd often drop pocketfuls of loose type (called "pi" in the printing business) on the ground. Considering that the simplest explanation makes the most sense, I'd vote for the latter. Or maybe both are true.

Notorious swindler and conman Charles Ponzi had an office off the alley.

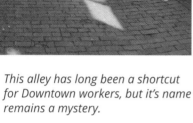

This alley has long been a shortcut for Downtown workers, but it's name remains a mystery.

PI ALLEY

WHAT Mysteriously named alley

WHERE 275 Washington St.

COST Free

PRO TIP Hungry for pizza pie, now? You can get a slice at a restaurant in the alley.

POLITICS AS USUAL

What nickname for a political dirty trick was coined in Boston?

Boston has many things to be proud of—this isn't one of them. On February 11, 1812, Massachusetts Governor Elbridge Gerry signed into law a bill that gave his party a clear advantage by shifting the borders of the state's congressional districts. The shape of Gerry's own home district, covering parts of the North Shore, was particularly odd. It appeared to resemble a salamander.

The *Boston Gazette* is credited with forever linking Gerry with the deceptive practice in an article on March 26, 1812: "The horrid Monster of which this drawing is a correct representation, appeared in the County of Essex, during the last session of the Legislature," read the *Gazette* article. "All believe it a creature of infernal origin, both from its aspect, and from the circumstance of its birth. . . . The Devil himself must undoubtedly have been concerned, either directly or indirectly in the procreation of this monster, yet many powerful causes must have concurred to give it existence. ... The monster shall be denominated a Gerry-mander."

Today, passersby can see a plaque describing the shady practice and a picture of the district downtown. The plaque reads:

> *The Gerrymander*
> *Near this site stood the home of state senator Israel Thorndike, a merchant and privateer. During a visit here in 1812 by Governor Elbridge Gerry, an electoral district was oddly redrawn to provide advantage to the party in office. Shaped by political intent rather than any natural boundaries, its appearance resembled a salamander. A frustrated member of the opposition party called it a gerrymander, a term still in use today.*

The Gerrymander

Near this site stood the home of state senator Israel Thorndike, a merchant and privateer. During a visit here in 1812 by Governor Elbridge Gerry, an electoral district was oddly redrawn to provide advantage to the party in office.

Shaped by political intent rather than any natural boundaries, its appearance resembled a salamander. A frustrated member of the opposition party called it a gerrymander, a term still in use today.

One of the tricks of the political trade, which earned its name here, is marked by this sign in Boston.

GERRYMANDER PLAQUE

WHAT Description of a term of political deception

WHERE The plaque hangs from a building on the corner of Arch and Summer Sts.

COST Free

PRO TIP For more fun and games in politics, head to the Old State House to see the so-called "Democratic Donkey" and Republican response (see page 38)

While Gerry certainly wasn't the first politician to use such a tactic, the gerrymander title has stood the test of time, as has the habit of politicians trying to game the system.

Gerry, who was born in 1744 and died in 1814, is also known for being a signer of the Declaration of Independence and the fifth vice president of the United States (1813–14) in the second term of President James Madison.

SPECIAL REQUEST

Can you really tweet to the Fenway Park organist to play a song?

Fenway Park is one of the few ballparks in the country with a live organist playing during the games. Since 2003 Josh Kantor has been the Fenway Park organist, a job requiring that he be a master multitasker.

He has to handle several different voices in his headset detailing what's happening during the game at any given point, coordinating musical choices with the park's DJ, listening to the engineers, watching the game, and minding the timing of the commercial breaks, not to mention having any number of songs on tap in his head and, of course, actually playing the organ.

In addition, several years ago Kantor decided to make his challenging job even more so when he began accepting song requests in real time on Twitter.

"I think I make it harder than it needs to be by taking the song requests," said Kantor, whose Twitter handle is @jtkantor. "But I do it to make things more fun for the fans and to make things more challenging and fun for myself."

During any given game, he's listening to, and sometimes learning, a few songs on the fly, then playing them. He says people are often surprised to find out that there is live organ music at all.

"People assume it is recorded music," he said. "And then they are pleased it is a real live person playing that music."

Last year Kantor fulfilled 738 fan requests. He usually publishes his list after the season ends.

At Fenway Park, fans can request songs from the live organist via Twitter.

TWEET REQUESTS AT FENWAY PARK

WHAT Get the organist to play your favorite song

WHERE Fenway Park

COST Free

PRO TIP Kantor shares musical duties with the park's DJ, TJ Connelly, who also DJs for the Patriots.

ANOTHER BRICK IN THE . . . GROUND

Where is one of Boston's most underrated artworks?

There is an utterly unique and charming piece of Boston artwork that gets stepped on every day, usually by people who don't even notice it. But when someone stops, slows down, and bends to look at the ground on Winthrop Lane, all the people rushing past stop and look, too, curious about what's down there.

What they see is nearly one hundred brick-sized reliefs in bronze installed seemingly haphazardly among the other bricks of Winthrop Lane, telling a tale of Boston's history, highlights, monuments, and much more.

Called *Boston Bricks, A Celebration of Boston's Past and Present*, the project was underwritten by the Browne Fund in Boston and A. W. Perry and Ryan Associates, created by artists Kate Burke and Gregg LeFevre, and installed in 1985.

Scenes run the gamut from the serious, like the Boston Tea Party and the Underground Railroad, to the funny, like a high-heeled shoe, which pays homage to Boston's now-defunct red-light district, the Combat Zone, and a monster behind the wheel of a car, perhaps a nod to Boston's reputation for bad drivers. There's even a scene of the famous Smoots prank by MIT students (see page 82).

Cultural institutions are well represented too, with a ballet slipper for the Boston Ballet, a flute for the Boston Symphony Orchestra, and a Verdi program, ticket stubs, and looking

BOSTON BRICKS

WHAT Playful homage to Boston

WHERE Winthrop Lane

COST Free

PRO TIP Look down!

This unusual art installation is often overlooked, but it is a creative and fun homage to Boston.

glasses for Boston's opera scene. The Boston Marathon, First Night, and Swan Boats also are depicted. It's definitely worth a detour from the Freedom Trail to check them out.

If you don't have time to check out all the bricks or if too many people get in your way, you can get a closer look on the artist's website at katekburke. com/section/143743-Boston-Bricks.html.

UNDERGROUND ART

Where can you see a highway underpass transformed?

Underground at Ink Block, located in an underpass between Boston's South End and South Boston neighborhoods, is one of Boston's more creative uses of a normally ignored and avoided section of a highway—its underbelly.

The eight-acre urban park, which came to fruition in 2017, links various neighborhoods via pedestrian boardwalks and bicycle paths. A major highlight of the whole area is the Underground Mural Project, which also launched in 2017. For the initial group of nine murals, street artists from Boston and across the country, including Vyal One, Upendo, Thy Doan, Problak, Percy Fortini Wright, Marka27, Imagine876, Hoxxoh, Ewok, Don Rimx, Cey Adams, and Andrew Balboa, were invited to transform 150,000 square feet of concrete walls, columns, and even the ground under the highway into colorful pieces of art.

In addition to the creative art, pop-up fitness classes, food trucks, festivals, and other community events help bring life to the cityscape. Instead of sitting unused as a sketchy section of town, the underpass takes advantage of the space in an unusual way, one that benefits the community.

In 2019, nine more murals were added to the Underground Mural Project, bringing the number of murals to eighteen. And this time, the artists, who included Dana Woulfe, Geo Go-Five, Greg Lamarche, Indie184, Marka27, Matthew Zaremba, Muro, and Silvia Lopez Chavez, came from around the globe.

The murals comprise one of the largest installations of public street art and infrastructure engagement in New England.

The murals at Underground at Ink Block help to transform a usually overlooked space into a cool destination.

MURAL PROJECT

WHAT Art under a highway

WHERE 90 Traveler St.

COST Free

PRO TIP The Broadway MBTA subway stop is steps away.

TRUE COLORS

Did the Red Sox really patent paint colors?

Several years ago, the Boston Red Sox worked with Benjamin
Moore to create The Fenway Collection, five ready-mixed colors
in a limited edition that matched those from America's oldest
ballpark. The partnership makes sense, considering that Benjamin
Moore is the official paint of the Red Sox and supplies the park
with its signature colors.

The collection includes Green Monster 12, Boston Blue 09,
Boston Red 42, Baseline White 08, and Foul Pole Yellow 27. And
because this involves baseball, of course each of the numbers was
selected for a specific reason:

Although Green Monster 12 is for Fenway Park's 1912 opening
year, the other color numbers commemorate the jersey numbers
of Red Sox greats: Ted Williams (Blue 09), Jackie Robinson (Red
42), Carl Yastrzemski (White 08), and Carlton Fisk (Yellow 27).

While the paint was supposed to be available for a short time
only, plenty of retailers still have it in stock, though you might not
see it on shelves. So, if you get inspired, you can create your own
Fenway Park-colored creation and know the colors are not mere
copies, but the real deal.

When the paint launched in 2014, Benjamin
Moore volunteers, retailers, and contractors
transformed Bunker Field in West Roxbury into a
mini Fenway Park.

Boston Red Sox fans can pick up the exact paint colors Fenway Park uses.

RED SOX PATENTED PAINT

WHAT Ultimate fan paint

WHERE Paint shops or online

COST Varies

PRO TIP Call to make sure your local store has it or can order it.

UNBROTHERLY LOVE

Did someone really build a house to spite his sibling?

Known as the "Skinny House" or the "Spite House," this ten-foot-wide house, located in the North End across the street from the Copp's Hill Burying Ground, is said to have been built as a rebuke from one brother to another.

According to local lore, in the 1800s two brothers inherited a plot of land from their father. One brother built a big house on the land while his brother was fighting in the Civil War. When the other brother returned to what little was left of the land, he built a home right outside his sibling's windows to block sunlight and the view of the harbor out of sheer spite.

The privately owned 1,166-square-foot, two-bedroom house is not open to the public, but in 2017 it went on the market, so all sorts of curious people—not necessarily would-be buyers—got a rare peek inside. Each floor is less than three hundred square feet in size.

On the first floor, there's a kitchen and a small dining area, plus a Juliet balcony. The second floor has a living room, bathroom, and another dining area. The third floor boasts a study and a bedroom with built-in bunk beds, and finally, there's a master bedroom that takes up the whole top fourth floor.

SPITE HOUSE

WHAT A ten-foot-wide house

WHERE 44 Hull St.

COST Free

PRO TIP This is a private residence. You can take photos, but don't trespass on the property.

This 10-foot-wide house was built out of spite.

This spite house isn't the only one. They can be found all over the world, sometimes painted in colors meant to intentionally irritate neighbors.

STICKY FLOOD OF DESTRUCTION

Did a molasses spill really kill twenty-one people?

Of all the ways to meet your end in the early part of the twentieth century, drowning in a tsunami wave of molasses was probably not at the top of anyone's list. Yet in January 1919, 21 people died, more than 150 were injured, and 25 horses were killed when a fifty-foot-tall steel tank filled with more than two million gallons of molasses came apart, releasing a fifteen-foot-high wave of destruction in Boston's North End. It raced at an amazing thirty-five miles per hour and destroyed everything in its path, including houses, businesses, and other buildings. It took more than six months to clean up.

What is now called the "Great Molasses Flood" was the result of haste, shoddy construction, and, no doubt, corporate greed. Built in 1915 by the Purity Distilling Company, which was owned by United States Industrial Alcohol, the tank held molasses that was used to produce industrial alcohol for liquor and munitions manufacturing and was in high demand during World War I. Located on Commercial Street, it almost immediately proved to be leaky and unstable, making groaning noises and seeping molasses. An employee warned the company that the tank was unsound, but nothing of import was done. In fact, the tank was painted brown to hide the leaks.

When the tank burst on January 15, 1919, the area was simply devastated. The combination of the warm molasses and the

For a comprehensive overview of the tragedy, pick up *Dark Tide: The Great Boston Molasses Flood of 1919* by Stephen Puleo.

One of Boston's strangest disasters is marked with a small sign in the North End.

cold temperature made rescue and clean-up a nightmare. It took days to recover some of the bodies and, in one case, four months. Despite trying to argue that the disaster was due to sabotage, the courts found the company at fault and ordered it to pay damages to victims.

GREAT MOLASSES FLOOD

WHAT One of Boston's more unusual tragedies

WHERE Commercial St., North End

COST Free

PRO TIP While there's no evidence left of the disaster, there is a small plaque describing the event on the 500 block of Commercial Street on a low wall next to Langone Park.

MODEL CITIZEN

Why is there a diorama of an Italian palace in the library?

A gorgeous and intricate diorama of the Palazzo Ducale, or Doge's Palace, is located at the public library in the North End. It has a long and convoluted history that is both sweet and a bit sad. The story starts with Henrietta Gardner Macy (1854–1927), a teacher and an artist who founded a kindergarten in the North End in 1878.

"Miss Macy," as she was known, eventually settled in Venice, Italy, and one summer she built a small model of the Doge's Palace for the sons of some visiting friends. The boys enjoyed helping her, but after returning home to Boston, they contracted diphtheria at school and died. Miss Macy was moved to build a larger model of the palace to honor their memories and for other children to enjoy.

After three years of work, the model was done and headed to New York, but it was destroyed in a fire en route. Miss Macy started anew and spent several years on another model but died in 1927 before it was finished. A friend of hers hired craftsmen to finish the model as a memorial to Miss Macy and then presented it to the North End Branch of the Boston Public Library.

The diorama recreates a lifelike scene from the sixteenth century and displays the sea-facing facade of the palace. The tiny figures, created by Miss Louise Stimson of Concord,

Look for the two fashionable ladies of the court inching their way along the dock; they are wearing shoes with wedge soles that translate to sixteen to eighteen inches tall in real life!

Created as a project to entertain visitors, this lovely model is a love letter to children.

Massachusetts, include artist Paolo Veronese and his wife strolling along the walkway, musicians setting up their instruments to begin a concert, and a widow who is husband-hunting in her black dress and gray veil, to name just a few. It's easy to picture the past looking at the diorama.

PALAZZO DUCALE DIORAMA

WHAT Detailed model of an Italian palace

WHERE North End Branch of the Boston Public Library, 25 Parmenter St.

COST Free

PRO TIP The library is closed on Sundays.

LABOR OF LOVE

Where can you find an alley covered in saints?

The North End, famous for its Italian heritage, dozens of tempting cafés and restaurants, and many historic sites, has plenty of diversions to offer, but there's one most visitors never see.

Located just off Hanover Street, in a gated alley on Battery Street that is usually kept locked, there's a surprising sight, the passion project of a single man, Peter Baldassari. For almost thirty years, Baldassari has collected thousands of images of saints and arranged them on the brick walls of the alley. Framed pictures and collages of Catholic saints, including religious cards, statues, crucifixes, and candles, cover the walls in a stunning display of faith.

Baldassari himself coined the phrase All Saints Way, which is a perfect name. His hobby began when he was a teen; he started collecting holy cards, which typically have a picture of a saint on one side and a prayer written on the back. After he got permission from the alley's landlord, he decided to create the shrine, which he has tended for almost three decades. He also decorates the gate outside at various holidays.

Above the door to All Saints Way, a sign says, "Mock all and sundry things, but leave the saints alone." If Baldassari happens to be around, he'll let you in to take a look, but even if he isn't, you can still see plenty.

ALL SAINTS WAY

WHAT A lifetime passion project

WHERE Battery St.

COST Free, but donations are accepted

PRO TIP The shrine is a work in progress. Feel free to bring a saint for Baldassari to consider.

This hidden-away alley pays tributes to saints.

Baldassari is something of a saint encyclopedia—it is said he can relate the story of every saint in his alley.

FOLLOW YOUR NOSE

What's down an alley and down the stairs in the North End?

It's easy to get distracted in the North End, what with all the enticing cafés, restaurants, bakeries, and gelato spots, but if you head down a narrow alley off Hanover Street, open the door marked "Fresh Artisan Breads," and walk down a set of stairs, you'll be rewarded with a pleasant, and tasty, surprise.

The heavenly scent of baking bread greets you, and then you have to make a hard decision: what kind of delicious bread should you buy? And how can you choose only one? There might be loaves of ciabatta with kalamata olives (hands down a crowd favorite) or prosciutto and Parmesan cheese, baguettes of all sizes, raisin bread, or sunflower batard. A sign above the counter reads, "Everything is done by hand with love and passion," and the breads definitely taste like it.

The tasty bakery is owned by local North End businessman Frank DePasquale, who also owns a string of restaurants, including Bricco Ristorante & Enoteca, AquaPazza, Mare Oyster Bar, Trattoria Il Panino, and several others. The bakery supplies all his eateries with bread, a pretty shrewd way to maintain a steady business, as well as selling to the general public.

It's a good idea not to be fixated on what breads might be available. The inventory changes at any given time but, after all, don't you want what just came out of the oven anyway? There are a few tables squeezed into the alley in case you want to tear into your bread immediately.

Right next door is Bricco Salumeria, where you can pick up all sorts of delicious accompaniments, including Italian meats, cheeses, and olives.

A hidden bakery is worth seeking out in an alley in the North End.

BRICCO PANETTERIA

WHAT Bread bakery

WHERE 11 Board Alley (behind 241 Hanover St.)

COST Varies

PRO TIP The store is open Sunday through Thursday from 6 a.m. to 8 p.m. and Friday and Saturday from 6 a.m. to 9 p.m.

ANTHONY! ANTHONY!

Is the old Prince Spaghetti commercial site real?

If you can remember the days before Netflix and on-demand cable shows, you might remember that some television commercials became instant pop-culture icons. One of these was filmed in the North End. You can still see where the pivotal scene was shot—it looks virtually unchanged since 1969.

The commercial, which ran for almost fourteen years, was for Prince Spaghetti and features a mother shouting out of an apartment window on Powers Court in the North End for her son, Anthony. The boy bolts home, racing through Haymarket, passing a bunch of men watching a bocce ball game and a schoolyard, as a narrator says:

"Anthony Martignetti lives in Boston, on Prince Street, in the Italian North End, the home for more than fifty years of the Prince Spaghetti Company. Most days, Anthony takes his time going home, but not today. Today is Wednesday, and as every family in the North End of Boston will tell you, Wednesday is Prince Spaghetti Day."

The twelve-year-old boy, whose real name actually is Anthony Martignetti, wasn't an actor and didn't even speak in the ad. It didn't matter. It made him famous, with people yelling "Anthony, Anthony" at him whenever they saw him. Martignetti still lives in Boston, but not in the North End. The fiftieth anniversary of the first airing of the commercial brought him into the limelight again.

The Prince Spaghetti Company started out of offices at 92 Prince Street in 1912. It eventually outgrew that space and later moved to Lowell.

Looking almost the same, this apartment building is the site of a famous commercial.

PRINCE SPAGHETTI COMMERCIAL SITE

WHAT Iconic window

WHERE The Exchange Building, Powers Ct.

COST Free

PRO TIP "Wednesday is Prince Spaghetti Day" was the company's official slogan.

BELOVED BILLBOARD

What's the story with this unlikely Kenmore Square icon?

Since 1965, an enormous sign advertising Citgo has sat atop 660 Beacon Street. The distinctive orange and red triangle in a white square is a landmark, a beacon, a way to orient yourself, and at night, a warm glow lighting up the night. It's graced countless postcards, books, and photos and is instantly recognizable as Boston.

Its future has waxed and waned, with the company, and even the building, changing hands over the years, but despite blackouts and near dismantling, it has endured. Bostonians keep fighting to keep the lights on.

We can be a superstitious lot, especially with regards to sports, and we like our traditions. Red Sox game attendees can see the sign from the first-base side in Fenway Park. In 2003 a malfunction caused the sign to go dark during the playoffs, which fans naturally blamed for the team's loss that year. In 2004, even though the sign was being worked on, the side facing the ballpark was left on, at the mayor's insistence. The Boston Red Sox won the World Series that year for the first time in eighty-six years.

It's also an important marker for Boston Marathon runners, who see it for the first time after completing the brutal Heartbreak Hill at Mile 20. When they pass it at Kenmore Square, they know they have only one mile to the finish line.

When the sign was built in 1965, it contained more than five miles of neon, but in 2005 the neon was converted to about 218,000 LED lights.

The fate of the Citgo sign has been precarious over the years, but it seems like the sign will be safe for some time. Photo courtesy Leise Jones.

CITGO SIGN

WHAT Giant sign

WHERE Kenmore Square

COST Free

PRO TIP The sign is best seen from a distance.

While the Boston Landmarks Commission lost a bid to get the sign declared an official city landmark in 2018, Citgo and developer Related Beal (which now owns the building) reached an "agreement in principle" on a lease to keep the sign in place for another thirty years. No doubt in three decades, there'll be a new crop of locals who will make sure it stays in place.

LONG LIVE THE RAT!

Where can you sleep in a suite dedicated to a closed nightclub?

Once upon a time, Kenmore Square was a less-than-savory area, with sketchy characters hanging out, trash on the sidewalks, and nothing much to recommend it. Except for the Rat, that is. A punk rock mecca, the Rathskeller (nobody called it that, though) was "the" place to play if you were in a band, usually before anyone ever knew your name.

Bands who played there include The Police, R.E.M., Talking Heads, The Romantics, Metallica—the list just goes on and on. It wasn't exactly an honor to play at the Rat, which was a dirty, sticky basement where you really didn't want to use the bathroom, but it was almost a rite of passage for up-and-comers. The Rat's run lasted for twenty-three years, closing in 1997 and ending an era.

Today, Kenmore Square is lively, bright, and safe, with the Hotel Commonwealth sitting in the place where the Rat once stood. As a tribute, the hotel features the Rathskeller Suite, which, rather ironically, is a luxurious spot to rest your head, but it still sports all sorts of memorabilia. Rat owner Jim Harold helped decorate it.

The one-bedroom suite sports the mirror, covered with band stickers, that once hung in the Rat's dressing room; drumsticks signed by Marky Ramone; a Cars guitar pick; and bathrobes with the Rat logo. It also has a bass that belonged to Ken Casey of the Dropkick Murphys (which guests can play)

For more Rat nostalgia, head to The Verb Hotel, where guests can see vintage band posters from the era.

While this old club is long gone, fans can relive their memories in a luxury hotel suite filled with memories. Photo courtesy Hotel Commonwealth.

and a plaid jacket from one of the Mighty Mighty Bosstones. And, of course, music of artists who played the Rat is available for listening, either on vinyl on a turntable or on a loaded iPod.

RATHSKELLER SUITE

WHAT Room dedicated to a defunct club

WHERE 500 Commonwealth Ave.

COST Varies

PRO TIP The hotel also has a Red Sox-themed suite, among others.

BOLD AS BRASS

Who stole thirteen pieces of artwork from the Isabella Stewart Gardner Museum?

One of the boldest and most notorious thefts in the art world happened in Boston on March 18, 1990. Two thieves dressed as police officers entered the Gardner Museum and stole thirteen works of art worth more than $500 million. To this day, it is the biggest unsolved art heist in history. The stolen pieces remain a heartbreaking loss for the world, with works by Rembrandt van Rijn, Johannes Vermeer, Edgar Degas, and Édouard Manet taken.

How the theft was carried out is now a well-known story. Early in the morning, the police impersonators pulled up near the employee entrance of the museum and told the guard they were responding to a call. The guard, breaking protocol, allowed them in. He and another guard were handcuffed, tied up, and left in the basement (they were freed by real police officers later that morning).

Because the museum had motion detectors, the thieves' movements were recorded and reconstructed. They first went to the Dutch Room and cut two Rembrandts from their frames: *Christ in the Storm on the Sea of Galilee* and *A Lady and Gentleman in Black*. Next they did the same with Vermeer's *The Concert* and Govaert Flinck's *Landscape with an Obelisk*, grabbed an ancient Chinese gu, or wine beaker, and removed a small self-portrait by Rembrandt from a chest.

The museum has a reward of $10 million for information leading directly to the recovery of all thirteen works in good condition. A separate reward of $100,000 is offered for the return of the Napoleonic eagle finial.

Left: *Edgar Degas's,* Leaving the Paddock (La sortie du pesage), *19th century watercolor and pencil on paper was one of the works of art stolen in the outrageous theft at the Isabel Stewart Gardner Museum in 1990. Photo courtesy the Gardner Museum.*

Right: *Rembrandt van Rijn's etching (about 1633),* Portrait of the Artist as a Young Man *was another of the stolen works. Photo courtesy the Gardner Museum.*

The thieves' next stop was the Short Gallery, where they took five Degas drawings and a bronze eagle finial. Their final destination was the Blue Room, from which they stole Manet's *Chez Tortoni*. Finally, the thieves made two trips to their car with the artworks and took off at 2:45 a.m. The entire episode, from start to finish, took eighty-one minutes.

Today, empty frames hang as placeholders for the missing art, which the museum hopes will be returned one day. Over the past three decades, the police and FBI have pursued many leads and the case remains active.

SECRET GARDEN

What's a don't-miss exhibit at the MFA that's not inside?

The Museum of Fine Arts, Boston has an enormous amount of art to take in, but if your senses get overloaded or your feet need a break, one of its most peaceful exhibits can be found outside. *Tenshin-En*, otherwise known as "Garden of the Heart of Heaven," was created in 1988 and named in honor of Okakura Tenshin, the Asian curator at the museum from 1904 until his death in 1913.

The garden was designed by Professor Kinsaku Nakane of Kyoto as a viewing garden in the *karesansui* style. Nakane said, "The goal of a *karesansui* garden is to suggest magnificent scenes from nature by forming the shapes of various landscape elements such as waterfalls, mountains, islands and ocean ... thus the garden expresses the vastness of nature in miniature, within a strictly limited space."

Though visitors don't need to know this to enjoy it, the garden's features include tall stones representing Mount Sumeru and two of the Mystic Isles of the Immortals: the Tortoise Island and the Crane Island. Cherry, Japanese maple, and pine trees are just a few of the species that grace the garden, ensuring that there is always something of nature to contemplate, no matter the season.

The garden's caretakers use a fifty-pound rake with eight tines to rake the gravel.

This rock garden offers a peaceful break from the bustling city. MFA_Photo © Museum of Fine Arts, Boston

TENSHIN-EN

WHAT Rock garden

WHERE 465 Huntington Ave.

COST Museum admission, $25

PRO TIP You can see the garden from the second floor of the West Wing, giving you a bird's-eye view and a different perspective.

RETRO ROCK-AND-ROLL DREAM

Where can you stay in a music-themed hotel?

The Fenway-Kenmore neighborhood didn't always look the way it does now. Today, it's packed with high-rises and high-end restaurants, but in the 1950s and '60s, it was the perfect place to open a modest motor inn. In 1959 the two-story Fenway Motor Hotel opened for business and proved quite popular. Entertainers like Connie Francis, Jerry Vale, and Tony Bennett all stayed at the hotel, with Bennett allegedly even performing one night in the cocktail lounge in a two-hour impromptu session.

The hotel was eventually turned into a Howard Johnson and finally closed in 2013. When new developers came in, the plan was to scrap it and start over, most likely to put another luxury property in its place, but fortunately that didn't happen.

Instead, paying homage to its original mid-century bones, developer Steve Samuels and hotelier Robin Brown created The Verb, with a funky, edgy design that embraces both the area's early ties to music and its currently thriving media and art scene. Everywhere you look, there are rare pop artifacts and music memorabilia, posters for clubs and bands (some long gone), and photos of breathtakingly young musicians, like Mick Jagger, in their heyday. It's a blast to just walk around and take everything in.

All the rooms feature record players and vinyl albums for you to play and rock out to (free earplugs if your neighbors are loud).

The lobby of The Verb Hotel feels like a rock star's living room. Photo by Rob MacKinnon.

The collection of items is courtesy of David Bieber, former archivist of the *Boston Phoenix*, a beloved alternative weekly (now defunct), who shares gems like backstage passes for the J. Geils Band, ticket stubs to a Blondie show at the Paradise, covers of old *Phoenix* issues, and much more.

THE VERB HOTEL

WHAT Hip hotel

WHERE 1271 Boylston St.

COST Varies

PRO TIP If you're not staying overnight, you can visit the hotel's bar instead and still enjoy the vibe.

Bright colors pop everywhere, from stained glass windows overlooking the pool to pink clocks in the rooms. Walking down the black-painted hallways makes you feel like you're in a nightclub—just the right touch for a hip hangout.

HE MEASURED UP

What is the deal with the painted lines on a bridge between Boston and Cambridge?

Lots of things have been invented in Boston and Cambridge, but maybe one of the quirkiest is the unit of measurement known as the "smoot." While it may sound vaguely scientific or official, a smoot, which equals five feet, seven inches, is actually the height of a former MIT student named Oliver R. Smoot.

SMOOTS

WHAT A college prank for the ages

WHERE Harvard Bridge

COST Free

PRO TIP The smoot has also been added as a unit of measurement on the Google calculator, so people around the world can use smoots to measure anything they want.

In 1958 the fraternity brothers of Lambda Chi Alpha decided to measure the bridge using, well, Smoot, who was a pledge with the fraternity. Not content to simply use a measuring tape or even a yardstick, the Lambda Chis laid Smoot down, head to toe, over and over, marking the bridge as they went. The final measurement totaled 364.4 smoots and one ear (or, as the rest of us would have it, 2,164.8 feet).

To this day, the fraternity repaints the smoot markings, and Smoot himself has returned for a few different celebrations, including the fiftieth anniversary of the prank. Lest you think this is just a funny local oddity, the smoot measurement has gained fame far beyond Boston and Cambridge. The story of its creation even inspired a book titled *Smoot's Ear: The Measure of Humanity* by Robert Tavernor.

Smoots are marked on both sides of the bridge, so it doesn't matter which side you walk along.

A prank played by MIT students more than 50 years ago lives on to this day.

MASTER PROMOTER

Did Houdini really jump off a bridge in Boston?

The Harvard Bridge, a.k.a the Mass Ave Bridge, might be more famous today for the smoots painted on it (see page 82), but long before that MIT prank was ever conceived, a much bigger spectacle packed the bridge with onlookers. It was the day the famous magician Harry Houdini performed one of his legendary feats.

Houdini had an upcoming show at Keith's Theatre, a vaudeville house, where, according to an ad in the *Boston Globe*, he would perform "New Feats of Daring and Skill, Including the Latest Mystery, His Escape From a Mammoth Can Filled with Water, In Which He Is Submerged, the Cover Being Locked With Six Padlocks." To ensure the performance was a success, Houdini planned an exciting preview.

On April 30, 1908, he jumped from the Harvard Bridge with his hands cuffed behind his back and chained to a collar around his neck. A policeman made sure the chains were secured. After a signal was tooted from a towboat, Houdini jumped off the bridge into the river and emerged forty seconds later, shackles in hand.

In a *Boston Globe* article titled, "Overboard Chained, Houdini Gets Free," the paper said about twenty thousand people showed up to see Houdini's stunt. As far as drumming

---

One of Houdini's more bizarre feats took place in Boston in 1911, when he was challenged to escape from an unidentified dead fifteen-hundred-pound sea creature, possibly a turtle. He was shackled hand and foot and inserted into the foul-smelling animal carcass, emerging fifteen minutes later.

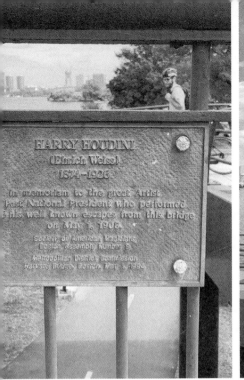

Magician Harry Houdini had a long history of performing stunts in Boston, including a famous jump off the Harvard Bridge.

up excitement for his two-week run at Keith's, it was pretty impressive.

Houdini, whose real name was Erik Weisz, emigrated from Hungary to Wisconsin with his family when he was four years old. When he was young, he was fascinated with magic and later changed his name in honor of his favorite magician, Jean-Eugène Robert-Houdin.

PUBLICITY STUNT

WHAT Site of a master magic trick

WHERE A plaque (with the incorrect date of the jump), is located on the Boston side of the Harvard Bridge, commissioned by Boston's chapter of the Society of American Magicians.

COST Free

PRO TIP Houdini died on Halloween in 1926, and his wife held seances every year for ten years trying to contact him.

WHALESPOTTING

Where is there a hidden whale mural in the South End?

For years, travelers heading down Route 93 could see a welcome and whimsical sight on the side of the Planet Self Storage building on Traveler Street: an enormous mural of a trio of killer whales in the ocean. Painted by Rhode Island artist Ronnie Deziel, the mural, which is 125 feet tall and 100 feet wide, also features dolphins and other sea life happily swimming around.

These days it takes a little more work to see the mural, which has been obscured from the highway by new construction in the popular neighborhood, but it's still possible to see the entire work on foot. Although he originally painted it in 1998, the artist redid it in 2015 after it was covered up for a couple years. He mostly stuck to the original design, but he did add a sperm whale and a sea turtle this time around.

Make sure to take a close look at the right side of the mural. You'll see the words "Welcome To" at the top, and with a little imagination, you can see fish spell out the word "Boston" vertically down the side.

KILLER WHALES MURAL

WHAT Almost-hidden mural on the side of a building

WHERE 33 Traveler St.

COST Free

PRO TIP The best way to see the mural is on foot.

If you are interested in seeing more murals, the 2019 Mural Project at the Underground at Ink Block is a short walk away.

Once an icon for drivers speeding down Route 93, you now have to get out of your car to see this whale mural.

TUNEFUL TEDDY (page 30)

TINY HOUSES (page 126)

HOT POT (page 42)

ALL ABOARD (page 132)

UNDERGROUND ART (page 56)

LIGHTING THE WAY (page 112)

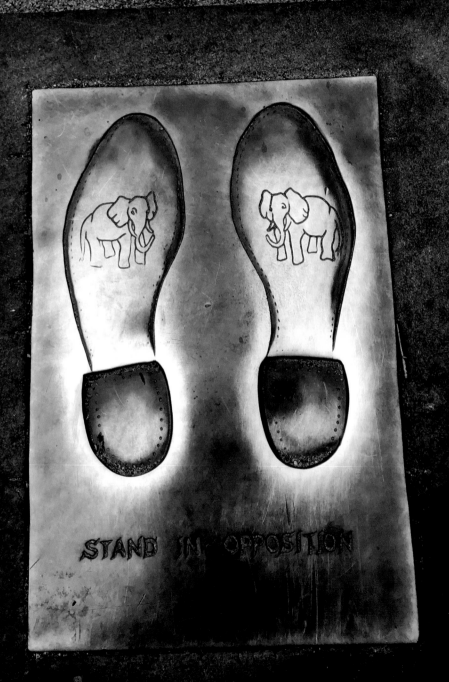

SHAPE-SHIFTER (page 106)

ANOTHER BRICK . . . IN THE GROUND (page 54)

8:14

9/11 TRIBUTE (page 164)

A RESCUE GONE AWRY (page 114)

Office →

HOME OFFICE (page 186)

BIRD'S-EYE VIEW (page 116)

THE CLAPP'S FAVORITE (page 140)

SHAPE-SHIFTER

Why does this sculpture get changed every year?

Typically, when a sculpture is created, it remains the same. A statue of a woman stays a statue of a woman; a monument of a globe stays a globe; a figure of an animal stays an animal. Not so with *Abstract Sculpture*, a steel-and-aluminum rhomboid dodecahedron split into two pieces, located in Armenian Heritage Park.

The sculpture, created by architect and designer Donald Tellalian, is dedicated to lives lost during the Armenian Genocide of 1915 to 1923 and subsequent genocides that have followed. Each spring, *Abstract Sculpture* is reconfigured (by crane) to create a new sculptural shape; the refiguring is meant to commemorate the immigrant experience and symbolize all who were pulled away from their country of origin and came to Massachusetts. The sculpture sits atop a reflecting pool.

While the sculpture is a dramatic statement, another highlight of Armenian Heritage Park is the Labyrinth, a winding circular path of stone inlaid in grass. The water of the reflecting pool reemerges as a single jet at the Labyrinth's center, a cycle meant to represent hope and rebirth.

The inscription on the Reflecting Pool reads in part: "The sculpture is offered is offered in honor of the one and one-half million victims of the Armenian Genocide of 1915–1923. May it serve in remembrance of all genocides that have followed, and celebrate the diversity of communities that have re-formed in the safety of these shores."

A unique aspect of this artwork dedicated to lives lost during the Armenian Genocide is that it changes annually.

ARMENIAN HERITAGE PARK

WHAT Moving monument to Armenian Genocide survivors

WHERE 115 Atlantic Ave. and Cross St.

COST Free

PRO TIP To learn more about Armenia, you can head to Watertown and visit the Armenian Museum, which boasts the largest collection of Armenian objects outside of the Republic of Armenia.

WHAT LIES BENEATH

What do Haymarket and a Roman floor have in common?

Haymarket, located just outside of Faneuil Hall, is one of America's oldest open-air markets. It's a bustling and lively spot to pick up fresh fruit and vegetables (just don't touch before you buy!) and has been a city staple for almost three hundred years. While there are plenty of things to catch your attention, make sure you look down!

Some of the scattered discards are not actually temporary; they are part of a bronze art installation called *Asaroton, 1976*. Artist Mags Harries, who also is behind the *Glove Cycle* (see page 188), describes the work like this:

"*Asaroton, 1976* focuses interest downwards to create an intimate experience of discovery. . . . The site hosts a famous open-air produce market. The embedded bronze pieces replicate the trash and debris that might normally cover the street. When the stalls and real debris of the farmer's market cover the art, it becomes part of a living experience. On the other days of the week it is a memory of the market."

ASAROTON, 1976

WHAT Installation art

WHERE Blackstone St. (between Hanover and North Sts.)

COST Free

PRO TIP The piece was commissioned as a commemoration of the Boston Bicentennial.

During the Big Dig, the installation was removed and relocated to the Museum of Science, where it remained for ten years. In 2006 a new *Asaroton* was installed at Haymarket.

An installation located underfoot is fitting tribute to Haymarket.

Harries drew inspiration from Roman floor mosaics called asaroton, which create the illusion of litter from a banquet, with items like fish heads and shells scattered about. The historic mosaics give insight into the ancient Roman world. Harries's work does the same for Boston, leaving a mark of another long tradition. The bronze pieces are set into concrete in a space of about fifty by ten feet.

REUSE, RECYCLE, RECREATE PART I

What island in the harbor used to be a garbage dump?

It may take a little time and effort to get to Spectacle Island, part of the thirty-four-island Boston Harbor Islands National Recreation Area, but the rewards are plenty: amazing views, a rich variety of summer programs, and even a beach. Over the centuries, the island has been used for fishing and hunting by native Americans, livestock grazing by Colonial settlers, an eighteenth-century quarantine station, and a popular place to have fun in the sun during the nineteenth century. In the early twentieth century, although it seems hardly possible now, the island had a garbage dump and a horse-rendering factory.

Like several other projects in Boston, the island's rehabilitation is thanks to the Big Dig construction project. Clay and sediment from the project sealed over the landfill, and over the years, amenities were added by the park service. Make sure you stop in the visitor center when you arrive to check out exhibits about

SPECTACLE ISLAND

WHAT Former landfill turned into a park

WHERE Boston Harbor Islands National Recreation Area

COST Free, but the roundtrip ferry costs $19.95

PRO TIP Ferry service runs from mid-May through mid-October.

Beachcombing for sea glass, pottery, and other debris is a popular activity, but you aren't supposed to keep anything you find. Turn in your treasures at the center and check out what other visitors have collected.

Spectacle Island, once a landfill, is now a great place to sunbathe and beachcomb.

the island's history. Spectacle Island offers five miles of trails to explore and a 155-foot-high viewing point, the highest in the islands, so don't forget to bring a camera.

Lifeguards are on hand in season to supervise the beach area, which is located close to the visitor center and ferry dock. Summer events include jazz performances on the porch of the visitor center, clam bakes, yoga classes, fishing clinics, kite-flying workshops, and much more.

LIGHTING THE WAY

Can you visit the oldest light station in the county?

Not only is Boston Light the oldest light station in the country at 303 years old, but it is also run by a woman—Sally Snowman—the light's first female keeper in its long history and the last resident lightkeeper in the US Coast Guard.

BOSTON LIGHT

WHAT Oldest lighthouse station in the United States

WHERE Little Brewster Island

COST Free, but the ferry is $19.95 roundtrip

PRO TIP The lighthouse was originally lit with candles!

The lighthouse tower was built by the British in 1716 and later destroyed by their forces during the Revolutionary War. It was rebuilt by the new American nation in 1783. In 1964 it became a National Historic Landmark, and in 1987 it was listed on the National Register of Historic Places.

The Coast Guard has phased out resident keepers at all light stations except for Boston Light because in 1989 the US Senate mandated that the Guard staff and keep the light accessible to the public in perpetuity, making it the only manned lighthouse in the United States. The light was the last in the country to be automated in 1998 and now is always "on," ending the days of a keeper having to climb the stairs twice a day.

Visiting Boston Light is a must for lighthouse fans. For Snowman and her husband, James Thomson, a volunteer assistant keeper, it's a way of life. Snowman, who holds two

Offseason or when the island is closed to visitors, you can take a two-hour Boston Harbor Lighthouse Tour, a cruise narrated by National Park Service and US Coast Guard staff.

Boston Light the oldest light station in the country and the last one to have a resident lightkeeper.

doctorate degrees and taught at Curry College in Milton, started volunteering there more than twenty years ago and became a paid civilian employee in 2004. The couple married on the island in 1994 and have written three books about the lighthouse. They live on the island from April to October.

A RESCUE GONE AWRY

Who is the Lady in Black?

Georges Island, one of the islands in the Boston Harbor Islands National Recreation Area, serves as the hub for visiting the other islands. On the thirty-nine-acre island, there's an excellent visitor's center, where you can watch a brief movie about the island's history, several trails, and of course, historic Fort Warren.

The fort, a National Historic Landmark, was built in 1833 and has served as a training ground for troops, a patrol point in the harbor, and a Civil War prison over the years. It's an intriguing place to spend some time, with any number of dark passageways and endless rooms to investigate. It's also home to a famous ghost.

As legend has it, in 1862 a Confederate soldier imprisoned on the island wrote home to his wife, Mrs. Melanie Lanier, who lived in Georgia. The devoted Mrs. Lanier hatched a plan to free her husband. After making the long trip from Georgia to Massachusetts, she rowed out to the island one night, dressed as a man and sporting a short haircut. She carried with her a pickaxe and a pistol.

Mr. Lanier guided her ashore, with the help of several sympathetic Confederate soldiers, by humming a familiar Southern song. She slipped through the bars and planned to dig him out, but they were discovered by a Union guard.

In season, rangers give twice-daily talks at "The Dark Arch" about Mrs. Lanier. Afterwards, you can explore the dark tunnel if you dare.

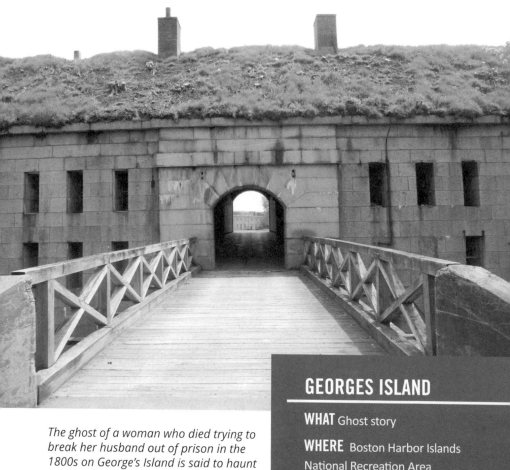

The ghost of a woman who died trying to break her husband out of prison in the 1800s on George's Island is said to haunt the grounds.

GEORGES ISLAND

WHAT Ghost story

WHERE Boston Harbor Islands National Recreation Area

COST Free, but the roundtrip ferry costs $19.95

PRO TIP Bring a flashlight for exploring dark passageways.

Mrs. Lanier held the guard at gunpoint, but he lunged for the pistol, which went off, accidently killing Mrs. Lanier's husband.

For all her efforts, Mrs. Lanier was sentenced to death by hanging. Her final request was to die in women's clothing, but black robes were the nearest they could come to that on the island. She was executed and buried on the island in the robes.

Since then, visitors have reported seeing a mysterious woman wandering the grounds of the island in black robes, so keep a sharp eye out.

BIRD'S-EYE VIEW

What hotel used to be the Custom House and was Boston's first skyscraper?

A Marriott hotel timeshare property seems like the unlikely custodian of one of Boston's most beautiful and historic properties, yet the domed Greek Revival building, completed in 1847, is still part of the cityscape. The tower was built later because of Boston's increasing shipping commerce—the water came right up to the tower at the time, and the added height allowed customs officials to ensure that no ships were slipping past without paying duty.

In 1913 the city exempted itself from local height restrictions of the time and financed a new five-hundred-foot-tall tower. It featured copper-sheathed couplet windows, an illuminated observation deck on the twenty-sixth floor, and twenty-two-foot-wide marble-and-bronze clocks on each of its four sides.

The outdoor deck wraps around the building and offers stunning 360-degree views, if you can get access. The Marriott does allow non-guests to enjoy the deck, but the hours are erratic, though they are usually in the afternoon. It is definitely worth figuring out when the deck is open in order to take in the views. A standout feature of the tower is its gorgeous four-sided clock, which can be seen from across the city and is especially beautiful at night. The clock ticked for the first time on April 6, 1916, at noon.

The tower, designed by the architectural firm Peabody and Stearns, was added between 1913 and 1915, making the building Boston's tallest until 1964.

The Custom House, Boston's first skyscraper, offers stunning views from its Observation Deck.

CUSTOM HOUSE DECK

WHAT Observation deck

WHERE 3 McKinley Sq.

COST Free

PRO TIP Call ahead, as the Marriott seems to change the deck's public access hours on a whim.

The original US Custom House was built with granite from the Pine Hill quarry in Quincy, and the grand rotunda was finished with Berkshire County white marble. Over the years, the building was used by different government agencies and finally closed in 1986. Marriott acquired it in 1997.

DAIRY KING

Why is there a giant milk bottle outside the Boston Children's Museum?

Located outside the Boston Children's Museum is a forty-foot-tall building in the shape of a milk bottle that usually houses an ice cream stand and snack bar (in 2019, it was not open). The story of the attraction and how it landed where it is today is a classic Massachusetts tale of scrappy enterprise and never letting anything go to waste.

The Milk Bottle was built in 1933 in Taunton, Massachusetts, by Arthur Gagner, who created it as roadside attraction in which he could sell his homemade ice cream. By 1943, the bottle was in the hands of the Sankey family, who sold ice cream purchased from dairy company H.P. Hood and Sons (hence the logo on the bottle).

By 1967 the Milk Bottle had been abandoned, and it sat empty and neglected for eight years. The next owner was the Rough and Ready Underwear Company, who wanted to donate it to the city of Boston. When City Hall was dismissed as an option, the Children's Museum became the next choice.

In April 1977, the Hood Milk Bottle arrived at the Children's Wharf like Cleopatra on a barge escorted by two fire boats. The excursion became known as "The Great Bottle Sail."

Since then the bottle-shaped building has been "de-capitated" and rebuilt to accommodate the move to the Children's Museum Plaza. Exactly thirty years after the initial relocation, Mayor Thomas Menino dedicated the building with its newly

---

Fun fact: if this were a real milk bottle, it would hold 58,620 gallons of milk!

This iconic giant bottle of milk was built in 1933 as a big ad and a place to sell ice cream.

replaced cap in 1977 to welcome it to its permanent home in the new Plaza.

GIANT HOOD MILK BOTTLE

WHAT Forty-foot-tall snack bar

WHERE 308 Congress St.

COST Free to see

PRO TIP If you're hoping to get a snack at the Milk Bottle, call ahead to see if it's open.

119

AEROSMITH SLEPT HERE

Don't you want to walk this way?

Once upon a time, in the early 1970s, Steven Tyler, Joe Perry, Tom Hamilton, Joey Kramer, and Brad Whitford were just like anyone else in Allston, living in one of the thousands of apartments occupied by college students and young people, happy with the cheap rents and proximity to the Green Line.

Of course, they weren't, and aren't, like anyone else. After Tyler happened to catch Perry and Hamilton playing with their band in August 1969 in Lake Sunapee, New Hampshire, their lives soon changed.

The next summer, the trio decided to form a band, and Tyler, who lived in New York City, joined Perry and Hamilton in Boston, where they had moved in 1970. Joey Kramer, who had gone to school with Tyler back in New York, joined up next. The Berklee School of Music student came up with the idea for the band's name—Aerosmith. Finally, Brad Whitford joined in 1971, and shortly thereafter, the group was a household name.

Happily, though, they never forgot their Boston roots. The 2012 unveiling of the plaque noting where they had lived happened to coincide with the launch of their album *Music from Another Dimension*, and the band came out to rock the neighborhood. Visitors can check out the plaque outside of 325 Commonwealth Avenue, where they lived from 1970 to 1972 and are said to have written some of their earliest hits, including "Movin' Out," written about leaving their second-floor abode.

AEROSMITH PLAQUE

WHAT Former apartment of rock legends

WHERE 1325 Commonwealth Ave.

COST Free

PRO TIP The apartment is private property, so just admire it from the outside.

The former home to the so-called "Bad Boys of Boston" is commemorated with a plaque.

Aerosmith Apartment

The five original members of the rock band Aerosmith (Steven Tyler, Joe Perry, Brad Whitford, Joey Kramer, and Tom Hamilton) lived on the second story of this building in the early 1970s. It was here "The Bad Boys of Boston" began their remarkable career. "Movin' Out," a track on their self-titled debut album, was written about moving out of this apartment. Known for their oversized personalities and combustible stage performances of blues-tinged hard rock, Aerosmith went on to become one of America's most influential rock and roll bands and achieved international success.

The band performed a six-song set list at the mini-concert, including favorites such as "Back in the Saddle," "Walk this Way," and "Sweet Emotion."

THE PLAY'S THE THING

Where is America's oldest community theater located?

Located on a side street in Jamaica Plain, sandwiched between two houses, is an unexpected attraction—America's oldest community theater. The Footlight Club has produced shows every year since 1877.

The idea of a theater club was proposed by Caroline Morse to several of her friends at a meeting she held at her home on Pond Street in December of 1876. In January, a more formal meeting was held, and in the end, twenty-five founders, all from wealthy and well-connected families, launched the club with the aim to "to promote friendly and social intercourse, and to furnish pleasant and useful entertainment by the aid of the drama."

While the group committed itself to produce a play in February, it had yet to come up with a name. Options included "Footlight," "Jamaica Plain," or "Jabberwocky." By the end of January, the group had found and rented a hall and decided upon a name. The club was so popular and shows so packed that it quickly outgrew its small space.

In 1878 the Footlight Club moved into Eliot Hall, renting the space from the First Parish Church (located across the street). The church was originally built in 1832 in Greek Revival/ Italianate style. In 1889 the club almost lost its home when the church decided to raze the hall. The Friends of the Club booster organization was able to raise the money to purchase the property. They converted the hall into a true theater,

Not only was the theater group founded in 1877, but Trinity Church in Copley Square was dedicated that year and the Swan Boats were first launched.

The Footlight Club is America's oldest community theatre.

and on January 9, 1890, the club's fiftieth production was performed in the new Eliot Hall. In the 1980s the building was again in bad shape, but once again people stepped up to save it. In 1988 it was added to the National Register of Historic Places.

FOOTLIGHT CLUB

WHAT Oldest community theater in the United States

WHERE 7 Eliot St.

COST Tickets vary

PRO TIP The theater generally offers shows September through May.

CAN'T SIT HERE

What's up with the crazy-looking bench at Jamaica Pond?

Strolling around Jamaica Pond, one of the gems in Boston's Emerald Necklace, visitors encounter runners, walkers, and families pushing strollers as they enjoy the scenery and get some fresh air. Ducks, turtles, and boats float in the pond's water. A gazebo and benches set all along the path offer places to sit or reflect.

All but one, that is. A very curious bench, one that is shaped like the letter U, is not exactly made for sitting. At first glance, it looks like every other wooden bench with metal legs in the park, but a doubletake makes it clear you're not seeing things.

Local artist and Massachusetts College of Art and Design professor Matt Hinçman installed the bench there in 2006, without permission from anyone. It lasted about a week before the city realized it wasn't one of theirs and removed it. But, in one of those rare happy-ending stories, the city asked him to get approval for the piece from the Boston Art Commission, which he received, and it was restored. Jamaica Pond Bench has been there ever since, a whimsical piece of art, one which the flexible can enjoy with a little effort.

Hinçman still gets up to his guerrilla art acts, including secretly installing a medallion on an old, broken lamppost at the corner of Eliot and Centre Streets in Jamaica Plain that depicts a hoodie to memorialize the murdered Trayvon Martin.

U-SHAPED BENCH

WHAT Art stunt

WHERE Jamaica Pond

COST Free

PRO TIP The artist was chosen by the City of Boston to create a new work for the nearby Jamaica Plain library. Plans are still underway, but it should be cool.

Top: *This quirky bench at Jamaica Plain invites speculation and was a guerilla artwork which the city embraced. Photo by Elizabeth Seitz.*

Inset: *Another hidden-in-plain-sight artwork by the same artist is located in Jamaica Plain.*

TINY HOUSES

Why does Forest Hills Cemetery have a village of miniature houses tucked into a hillside?

Historic Forest Hills Cemetery is not merely a burial place—it is one of the most famous garden cemeteries in the country. Founded in 1848, the 275-acre property is on the National Register of Historic Places and offers a beautiful place to wander. It is also an open-air museum, and artwork can be found everywhere, if you know where to look.

Since its founding, the cemetery has been home to art—in fact, it predates the Museum of Fine Arts, Boston by a good twenty years! It has always had sculptures for the public to enjoy, along with its winding paths and relaxing shady nooks. While there are plenty of Victorian sculptures to admire, there is also contemporary artwork.

In 2001 the Forest Hills Educational Trust established the Contemporary Sculpture Path. Visitors can pick up a map of the path at the entrance to the cemetery. One of my favorites is a hidden gem called *Neighbors 2006*. The artist, Christopher Frost, created a mini-village of concrete houses which replicate, albeit in small scale, the homes of several people buried in the cemetery. Their occupations, including grocer, merchant, and lead manufacturer, are etched into the homes, which are in different architectural styles, such as Queen Anne and modern split level.

Visit Christopher Frost's website (christopherfrost.com) to see more of his work around town.

One of America's most beautiful garden cemeteries is also home to a variety of art.

The houses represent the residences of Charles Varney Whitten (1829–1897), merchant; Mary Hunt (1830–1906), temperance leader; John A. Fox (1836–1902), architect; Joseph H. Chadwick (1827–1902), industrialist, whose Gothic Revival mausoleum is on Fountain Avenue; Ralph Martin (c. 1898–1919), wagon driver, who perished in the Great Molasses Flood; Samuel S. Pierce (1807–1881), grocer; and Anne Sexton (1928–1967), poet.

ON THE FLIP SIDE

Where is there a hidden record store in the back of a restaurant?

If you didn't know about it already—or never had to visit the restrooms—you might think Tres Gatos restaurant in the Jamaica Plain neighborhood of Boston was just another restaurant. You'd be wrong.

Tres Gatos not only serves up delicious Spanish tapas, pinchos, and paella, but it also has a record and bookstore tucked away in the back. Filled with old and new labels and books, it's an ideal place to while away time if you have to wait for a table (or even if you don't). As far as I know, it's a one-of-a-kind spot in the city. Tres Gatos, which opened in 2011, took over the space from Rhythm & Muse, a book and record store, and decided to keep selling albums and books in back. With fewer and fewer brick-and-mortar spots to buy such treasures, it's a neighborhood gem.

The excellent staff will happily discuss music, look up titles, and special-order anything you might want. And if you can get out of the shop without being tempted by the dishes coming out of the kitchen, you're a stronger person than I am.

The store stays open until the last bar or restaurant patron leaves, so you can shop well into the wee hours, long after most stores close.

Head to Tres Gatos' back room to discover a record and bookshop.

TRES GATOS

WHAT Hip shop in the back of a restaurant

WHERE 470 Centre St.

COST Free to browse

PRO TIP The shop offers book signings and author events, so check its calendar for info.

BONSAI BONANZA

Why are there tiny trees in a shade house in the Arboretum?

The Arnold Arboretum, one of the parks in the Emerald Necklace, has 281 acres of green space to explore, with everything from lilacs to rhododendrons to hemlocks to enjoy, depending upon the season. One of its more distinctive and rare collections is the Larz Anderson Collection of Japanese Dwarfed Trees, which can be seen in the spring and summer only.

The bulk of the collection—originally imported into the country by the Honorable Larz Anderson in 1913 after he returned from serving as ambassador to Japan—was donated by Isabel Anderson in 1937, after her husband passed away. She also donated the money for a shade house for their display (see page 182 to learn about another of the Larz family's collections). Over the years, more trees have been added to the collection, so there are now thirty-nine curated specimens, some as old as an astounding 275 years. The stars of the collection are six hinoki cypresses, or Chamaecyparis obtusa, which are quite rare, even in Japan.

While bonsais can be left outdoors in winter in most of Japan and parts of the United States, New England's winters are too cold, so the collection gets tucked away in a concrete-block building that is maintained at thirty-three to thirty-six degrees Fahrenheit. You can find the collection near the Dana Greenhouses, overlooking the Leventritt Shrub and Vine Garden.

On select Thursdays and Sundays, the pavilion is open and visitors have the chance to get closer to the collections. Volunteers are on hand to answer questions.

Only in public view in warm weather, the Arnold Arboretum's bonsai collection features tiny trees as old as 275.

THE BONSAI & PENJING COLLECTION

WHAT A tiny forest of trees

WHERE Arnold Arboretum

COST Free

PRO TIP The bonsais are only out seasonally (usually) when it is warm enough. Call ahead to see if they can be seen.

ALL ABOARD

Where can you find a bunch of adults playing with model trains?

Tucked away on the second floor of a building in Roslindale is a magical world, one you'd never guess was there from simply walking by. The Bay State Model Railroad Museum was established in 1968 in Roslindale by a local model railroad club. In 1977 the club was evicted from its original space, but with a massive effort, it managed to buy its new location, ensuring that no landlord could ever raise the rent or kick the group out. That's always a risk for model railroad clubs who rent space. They can lose years of meticulous hard work at the whim of someone who is not invested in the idea.

Today at the club, scale models (O, N, HO, and HOn3) depict scenes from all across the Unites States, including some very familiar areas in and around Boston. Most layouts represent tableaus from the 1930s to the 1950s. A replica 1940 Roslindale Square, the home of the club and museum, offers a charming peek into the past. Besides the historically accurate trains, there are also all sorts of vintage automobiles to check out, as well as tiny figures engaged in various activities.

From the fall foliage colors in some scenes to period advertisements posted on stores, the attention to detail is among the reasons people flock to the museum club's open

The railroad club/museum is open to the public twice a year for open houses, once in the spring and once in December. Check its website for details.

This model railroad club has been building trains since 1968. The public can get a peek during a couple of annual events.

houses, which are few and far between. It's easy to get absorbed watching the members work on projects, run trains, and explain how their world works.

BAY STATE MODEL RAILROAD MUSEUM

WHAT Longtime model railroad club/museum

WHERE 760 South St., Roslindale

COST Free

PRO TIP If you can't wait for an open house, call and ask if you can visit. A member might take pity on you and invite you in.

TRAIN WRECK

What tragedy helped to change the way bridges are built?

On March 14, 1887, a commuter train making its way from Dedham Station to Boston, with scheduled stops in West Roxbury, Roslindale, and Forest Hills, never finished its normally routine journey.

Instead, as the train approached the Bussey Bridge, located over South Street in Roslindale, the structure began to collapse as the last six of the nine passenger cars traversed it. The wooden coach cars crashed forty feet to the ground, shattering into pieces. When the conductor realized what happened, he raced the train ahead with the remaining cars to Forest Hills to get help. In the end, it was estimated that 23 passengers were killed and at least 125 injured.

Bussey Bridge, so named for the Bussey family, who owned a nearby farm (that later became part of the Arnold Arboretum), was known as the Tin Bridge. In earlier days, as a wooden bridge, it was sheathed in tin to prevent it from catching fire. That bridge was replaced by an iron bridge, but the nickname stuck.

The "new" bridge was never built correctly and never inspected. It was basically a disaster waiting to happen, a fact that the Massachusetts Board of Railroad Commissioners discovered after an investigation. The tragedy did, however, lead to a significant change in bridge safety across the country, requiring certified engineers to conduct all inspections. Today, the bridge still carries trains across South Street, but it is built of stone and cement.

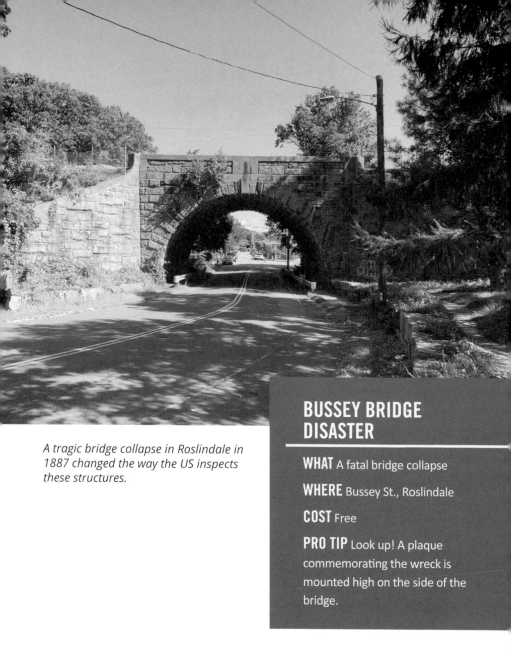

A tragic bridge collapse in Roslindale in 1887 changed the way the US inspects these structures.

Oddly enough, the disaster helped Roslindale grow; many onlookers came to see the notorious site, but then fell in love with the bucolic area and moved in.

REUSE, RECYCLE, RECREATE PART II

Where can you play on a (former) landfill?

Boston's Big Dig construction project had more impact than just burying an ugly highway underground. One of them, Millennium Park in West Roxbury, happens to be miles away from where the project took place.

The one-hundred-acre park is a busy hub of Little League games, families enjoying the playgrounds and fields, and picnickers. But it wasn't always such a charming scene. Once upon a time, it was a landfill. In 2000 the city used dirt from the Big Dig to cover the top of the landfill. A twenty-one-acre hill is home to the fields and other play spaces, while the rest of the grounds include wetlands, meadows, and wooded paths.

There's also a canoe launch right on the Charles River, an outdoor exercise station, a nature trail, and several miles of trails where you can walk, bike, or take your dogs for some exercise. The paved part of the trail inside the park is perfect for strollers, kids learning to bike, or those just taking in the natural beauty of the area, with commanding views of Boston, the Blue Hills, the river, and Newton. It's the perfect spot to fly a kite too.

MILLENNIUM PARK

WHAT A landfill turned into a park

WHERE 300 Gardner St., West Roxbury

COST Free

PRO TIP The park is open from dawn to dusk.

Bring a camera to capture great views of Boston's skyline.

Millennium Park, a former landfill in West Roxbury, is one of the happy benefits of the Big Dig.

While you can stick to the park, it is definitely worth going farther afield. A bridge across Sawmill Brook connects Millennium Park with the Oak Hill trails, which run through Brook Farm and connect to the Helen Heyn Riverway and Nahanton Park.

UTOPIAN DREAM

Where can you see the mid-nineteenth-century location of an experimental society of Transcendentalists?

These days, it might seem unlikely that West Roxbury was once home to an experimental utopian society inspired by the Transcendentalists, but such luminaries of the movement as Nathaniel Hawthorne, Ralph Waldo Emerson, and Margaret Fuller lived at and visited the farm in the 1840s.

Brook Farm, now a 179-acre National Historic Landmark, was established in West Roxbury in April 1841 by the Transcendentalists George and Sophia Ripley. Its lofty goal—to equally distribute the tasks of daily life, provide education for participants, and achieve a balance of work and leisure, all to benefit the greater good—proved to be unsustainable. Even though the farm produced a surplus, it never turned a profit, and it closed in 1847. It truly was a utopian dream.

Over the years, the land was used as a poor farm, a Civil War training ground, and, for seventy years, an orphanage, which closed in 1943. There is also a cemetery on the property now. While the main building is in disrepair and closed to the public, the lands are free to explore, with trails leading through fields, forests, marshes, and wetlands.

Nathaniel Hawthorne would later set his novel *The Blithedale Romance* in a utopian community modeled after Brook Farm.

Margaret Fuller

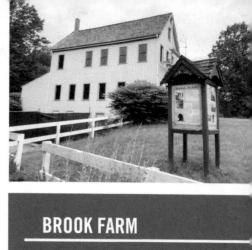

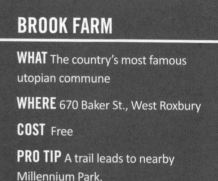

BROOK FARM

WHAT The country's most famous utopian commune

WHERE 670 Baker St., West Roxbury

COST Free

PRO TIP A trail leads to nearby Millennium Park.

Brook Farm was once home to Ralph Waldo Emerson, Margaret Fuller, and the famous experimental society of Transcendentalists in the 1840s.

THE CLAPP'S FAVORITE

Why is there a twelve-foot-tall pear sculpture in Dorchester?

Situated on a busy corner called Edward Everett Square in Dorchester is a unique sculpture, one which isn't the familiar ode to a war hero or a historic figure. Most people in the city might be surprised to learn that pears used to be grown in abundance in Dorchester and that one variety was even invented here.

The Clapp (sometimes spelled Clap) family was one of the founding families of Dorchester. Roger Clapp sailed from England on the *Mary and John* in 1630. In the 1830s, Harvard graduate Thaddeus Clapp, one of Roger's descendants, successfully cross-bred two popular varieties, the Flemish Beauty and the Bartlett, to create the Clapp's Favorite Pear, an early-ripening hit with consumers.

When artist Laura Baring-Gould was tapped to create public artworks in the square with subjects exploring Dorchester history, she was taken with the pear story and realized her vision with the twelve-foot bronze *Clapp's Pear*. On Saturday, June 16, 2007, Mayor Thomas M. Menino dedicated the sculpture.

Surrounding the pear are ten smaller bronze replicas of everyday objects honoring Dorchester's varied and unique history, including a pile of inscribed dog tags, an iconic three-decker house, a pair of Colonial-era shoes, and more, all inscribed with quotes from locals.

The Clapp's Favorite Pear variety is still grown today.

140

In the 1830s, pears were a big deal in Dorchester, where one family invented a hybrid that we can still eat to this day.

CLAPP'S PEAR

WHAT Giant fruit sculpture

WHERE 256 Boston St., Dorchester

COST Free

PRO TIP The nearby William Clapp House, where the Clapps farmed, is now the Dorchester Historical Society's headquarters.

HOPEFUL SIGN

Where can you find a gas tank painting designed by a former nun?

Boston is filled with iconic sights that most people simply take for granted, but some have more interesting backstories than others. One of these concerns the colorfully painted gas tank located in Dorchester, alongside the Southeast Expressway (Route 93).

The 140-foot-tall rainbow, commissioned by the Boston Gas Company in 1971, is the work of Corita Kent, a former nun-turned-artist. Her design, with its giant swaths of color, became the largest copyrighted artwork in the world.

Kent's story is a fascinating one. Born in 1918, she entered the religious order the Sisters of the Immaculate Heart of Mary at age eighteen. She worked as a teacher and then as the head of the art department at Immaculate Heart College in California. Over the years, most notably in the 1960s, her work became more political as she urged people to consider poverty, racism, and injustice. She left the order in 1968 and moved to Boston, where she continued to work on social causes. Her rainbow gas tank design (which was actually painted by professional sign painters) was meant to be a sign of peace and hope.

At the time of her death in 1986, she had created almost eight hundred serigraph editions, thousands of watercolors, and a huge number of public and private commissions. The nonprofit Corita Art Center, a project of the Immaculate Heart Community, preserves her legacy and promotes her work.

If Corita's art makes you happy, you can order anything from mugs to posters with her distinctive designs on the Corita website (corita.org).

A Boston landmark, the rainbow design on this gas tank, was actually created by a nun.

RAINBOW GAS TANK

WHAT Colorful art

WHERE Dorchester

COST Free

PRO TIP You can't actually visit the gas tank, which is fenced off, but it's best seen from afar anyway.

THIS OLD HOUSE, PART I

Where is Boston's oldest house located?

You might think Boston's oldest home would be in Beacon Hill or the North End, but you'd be wrong. It's actually located in Dorchester, about four hundred yards from its original location. Built in 1661, the James Blake House is named for its original owner, a minister who settled in Dorchester in the 1630s. Blake built the house in the Western English style, and it is now one of only a few examples of West England country framing in the United States.

Most of the early Colonial homes in Dorchester were built by housewrights from the south and east of England, where brick and plaster building predominated. What distinguishes the Western England style is the use of heavy timber-framing methods. The house, which is owned by the Dorchester Historical Society, has two stories with a central chimney and a gable roof.

The Blake House was once the main part of a ninety-one-acre estate that included a ten-acre home farm with at least two outbuildings and an orchard, yards, and a garden. James Blake did well for himself and held public office as a constable, town selectman, and deputy to the General Court. He also served as a Deacon of the First Church for fourteen years and later as a Ruling Elder. The house stayed in the family's hands for several generations. In 1895, it was sold the city, and the Historical Society then acquired it and moved it to its present location to save it from demolition.

The Dorchester Historical Society only offers tours of the house on the third Sunday of each month, from 11 a.m. to 4 p.m.

The oldest house in Boston, built in 1661, is located in Dorchester and is only one of a few examples of West England country framing in the United States

JAMES BLAKE HOUSE

WHAT Oldest house in Boston

WHERE 735 Columbia Rd., Dorchester

COST Free

PRO TIP The Dorchester Historical Society also manages two other historic houses in the neighborhood, the Captain Lemeul Clap House and the William Clapp House.

ZOO RELIC

Where can you see a long-abandoned zoo exhibit?

Franklin Park, one of the links in Boston's Emerald Necklace, was designed by nineteenth-century landscape architect extraordinaire Frederick Law Olmsted. The 485-acre park includes a plethora of green spaces, with woodlands, fields, playgrounds, a zoo, a golf course, and a delightful number of hidden and sometimes long-forgotten spaces.

One of these places is in Long Crouch Woods, a twenty-six-acre woodland section of the park. It has a wide main path through the middle and smaller trails leading into the woods. The Bear Dens, one of Franklin Park Zoo's earliest exhibits, is located here. The dens opened in 1912 and were permanently closed in 1971. Now, not even located within the boundaries of the zoo, the dens are abandoned and neglected, rusting and crumbling.

When you come upon them walking through Long Crouch Woods, they seem vaguely menacing. But don't run off in fright.

Stop and check out the rather intricate and pretty stone carvings on one of the walls. The frieze is of two standing bears holding up Boston's city seal and shows the 1912 Boston skyline with the Custom House, the tallest building in the city at the time. And if you do want to see some real bears, black bear brothers Bubba and Smoky reside in the much more humane Yukon Creek exhibit at the zoo.

BEAR DENS

WHAT Former zoo exhibits

WHERE Off Seaver St.

COST Free

PRO TIP There is parking on nearby Seaver Street.

Deep in Franklin Park, visitors can find the remains of bear dens, once an exhibit for the zoo.

The architect for the bear dens was Arthur Shurcliff (1870–1957), who started his career with Frederick Law Olmsted. The pair created a four-year program in landscape architecture at Harvard University, the first of its kind in the United States.

RESTORED RUINS

Did Ralph Waldo Emerson live in Franklin Park?

No, not exactly. Before Franklin Park was a city property, it belonged to several different owners. One of them, Jeremiah Williams, sold a five-and-a-half-acre parcel with commanding views to the city in 1882. This plot was formerly the home of the famous writer and Transcendentalist Ralph Waldo Emerson, who lived there in a cabin for two years from 1823 to 1825 while he was teaching in Roxbury.

When Frederick Law Olmsted learned of this fact while laying out the area, he named this section, located near the center of the park, Schoolmaster Hill in Emerson's honor. Olmsted designed several stone terraces so visitors could enjoy the expansive views. At one point in the early days of the park, the park superintendent's office was located here.

Now there are stone arches and pathways, picnic tables and benches overlooking the golf course. The structures look like the remains of a castle from long ago and are sure to ignite the imagination of children.

Make sure you walk under the arbor at the end of the walkway to see a plaque commemorating Emerson. It reads:

NEAR THIS ROCK
A.D. 1823–1825
WAS THE HOME OF SCHOOLMASTER
RALPH WALDO EMERSON

It also has a segment of his poem "Good-bye."

Emerson certainly upgraded his digs in 1835. You can visit his house, which is a National Historic Landmark, in Concord.

The locks allow boats to move back and forth from the Boston Harbor to the Charles River Basin.

RIVER LOCKS

WHAT River locks system

WHERE Near Paul Revere Park

COST Free

PRO TIP You may have to wait a while for a boat to come along and activate the lock.

BELLRINGERS

What's attached to the side of the pedestrian walkway in Charlestown?

As you walk along the sidewalk between Charlestown and North Station, there's a railing over the Charles River with odd handles sticking out. On the other side are what look like pieces of pipe welded to the fence. If you're not a curious person, you might just walk right on by and not realize what they are.

If you push the handles, they strike the pipes and musical tones ring out. In total, there are thirty tubular bells, each three inches in diameter, ranging in length from four to eight feet, and they're all part of an interactive musical sculpture called *Charlestown Bells*.

Installed in 2000, they are the creation of Groton artist Paul Matisse (who happens to be the grandson of the famous French painter Henri Matisse). The bells were commissioned by the Metropolitan District Commission. After succumbing to weather and perhaps overenthusiastic use, the bells stopping working some time later.

Two local Charlestown residents who loved the bells and missed them formed Friends of the Charlestown Bells in order to raise awareness to get them restored. The city kicked in the money, and Matisse, with the help of volunteers, uninstalled, repaired, and reinstalled them in 2013.

Matisse was commissioned to make *The Olympic Bell* for the 2004 Summer Olympic Games in Athens. The piece is now installed at Old Frog Pond Farm in Harvard, Massachusetts, as part of an outdoor sculpture exhibit.

CHARLESTOWN BELLS

WHAT Musical installation

WHERE Revere Park

COST Free

PRO TIP Another Matisse musical piece, called *Kendall Band,* was installed at the Kendall Square subway station in 1987.

Don't miss the unique musical installation on the dam by Revere Park, designed by Paul Matisse.

HOT POTATOES

Why is there a memorial dedicated to the humble spud?

"Potato, potato, potatoes, potato, potato, potatoes, potato, potato, potato, potatoes, potato, potato, potato," reads a plaque located next to a statue of—what else?—sacks of potatoes. Three closed sacks are topped by an open sack with spuds spilling out.

The Potato Shed Memorial pays homage to a time when massive potato sheds existed among the rail yards in Charlestown. The artwork is in a rather hidden place along the Millers River Littoral Way, just off a walkway next to a parking lot. Ross Miller, a visual artist, helped bring the piece into reality after hearing about the sheds when he was working on the Big Dig's Central Artery Arts Program in the 1990s.

The plaque says "millions and millions" of potatoes were shipped by rail from Maine from the mid-nineteenth century through the 1930s and off-loaded into the giant storage

POTATO SHED MEMORIAL

WHAT Quirky artwork

WHERE Millers River Littoral Way

COST Free

PRO TIP If you're driving, park at the far end of the Bunker Hill Community College parking lot.

You can find lots of Ross Miller's other projects around Boston and Cambridge. Visit his website to find out where (rossmiller.com).

156

This hard-to-find sculpture harkens back to the days when Charlestown was home to potato sheds.

warehouses and that "long-standing community members have first-hand memories of their trips to the sheds."

When a ten-alarm fire in May 1962 burned millions of pounds of stored produce set to be shipped throughout the East Coast, the whole area allegedly smelled like baked potatoes. The sheds were never rebuilt.

WHAT'S IN A NAME?

Should the Battle of Bunker Hill really be called the Battle of Breed's Hill?

The Bunker Hill Monument in Charleston, located on the Freedom Trail, is 221-foot-tall obelisk commemorating not a win for the Revolutionary forces, but a loss. It also might be misnamed, not that anyone really cares these days.

On June 17, 1775, at the start of the Revolutionary War, the British defeated the Americans at the Battle of Bunker Hill. Despite the loss, the inexperienced Colonial forces still managed to inflict significant casualties against the enemy, with the British sacrificing nearly half of their twenty-two hundred men. American casualties were numbered between four hundred and six hundred.

While the fight is commonly called the Battle of Bunker Hill, most of the actual conflict took place on nearby Breed's Hill. On the day before the historic battle, about one thousand Colonial militiamen under the command of Colonel William Prescott built earthen fortifications on top of Breed's Hill, which overlooked Boston from the Charlestown Peninsula. The troops were told to build the earthworks on Bunker Hill but instead chose Breed's Hill, which, although smaller, was closer to the city. And so, despite the actual site of the fighting, the battle was named for its originally planned location.

The monument's cornerstone was laid in 1825, but funds for construction ran out, and the project wasn't completed until 1842, when locals, many of them women, held fundraisers to raise money. The monument was finally dedicated in 1843.

Head to Bunker Hill to hear how a famous battle got its name. Photo credit: Boston USA

BATTLE OF BUNKER HILL

WHAT Misnamed battle

WHERE Charlestown

COST Free tickets are required to visit. Pick them up at the Bunker Hill Museum (located across the street from the monument grounds) in advance.

PRO TIP It is 294 steps to the top, but the views are worth the climb.

Bunker Hill Lodge, built next to the monument in 1901, features a statue of patriot and hero Joseph Warren, who was killed in the battle, as well as portraits and "The Adams," a famous Revolutionary-era cannon. Across the street from the monument's grounds is the Bunker Hill Museum, where exhibits explain more about the Battle of Bunker Hill, the monument and its construction, and historic Charlestown.

PLAY THE LOTTERY

Is it possible to sail on, not just tour, the USS *Constitution*?

Normally, the USS *Constitution*, better known as Old Ironsides, sits at its berth in the Charlestown Navy Yard and is open for tours, but on special occasions, such as the Fourth of July, the ship heads out into the harbor. And three hundred lucky people get to ride along.

They just have to win the lottery—the *Constitution* lottery, that is. Each spring, the Navy officially opens the lottery to the public for its July Fourth turnaround cruise. One hundred fifty winners, who can each bring a guest, get to ride aboard the *Constitution* in Boston Harbor. Passengers get to engage with active-duty sailors and learn about the ship's legacy, while sailing on a piece of history.

JULY FOURTH RIDE-ALONG ON THE USS *CONSTITUTION*

WHAT Lottery to ride Old Ironsides

WHERE Pier One, 55 Constitution Rd., Charlestown Navy Yard

COST Free

PRO TIP Typically, the lottery opens in March and the winners are announced in June.

The USS *Constitution* is the oldest commissioned ship in the US fleet. She was launched on October 21, 1797, as part of the nation's new navy. Her hull was made of live oak, the toughest wood grown in North America, and her bottom was sheathed in copper provided by Paul Revere. The nickname Old Ironsides

Don't miss the USS *Constitution* Museum just next door for more info and hands-on exhibits that kids (and many adults) love.

A lucky few can win a spot on Old Ironsides to sail on the Fourth of July.

was coined during the War of 1812, when shots from the British warship *Guerrière* appeared to bounce off her hull. In forty-two engagements, she never lost a battle, an impressive record. Today, she serves as America's Ship of State.

A HEAD FOR DISSENT

Did someone really saw off the USS *Constitution*'s figurehead?

Political protests in Boston have famously taken many forms, from throwing tea in the harbor to marching in the millions, but one of the city's stranger stories of expressing dislike for the powers that be took place about 185 years ago.

On the stormy night of July 2, 1834, Captain Samuel W. Dewey rowed out to Old Ironsides and sawed through the wooden figurehead of President Andrew Jackson that had been installed the previous year. Clearly, Dewey was not a fan of the president. Neither were many Bostonians, who disapproved of the president's veto of a certain bill.

It wasn't an easy job for Dewey. According to the *Constitution* Museum's website, "Dewey climbed up the ship's side by the man-ropes and ensconced himself in the bow . . . He extended himself on his back, and in this position sawed off the head. . . . Having completed his midnight decapitation Dewey regained his boat, to find her full of water . . . In this plight, but never forgetting the head he risked his life to obtain, Dewey reached the shore."

In 1847 Andrew Jackson once again graced the ship. The second Jackson figurehead resided safely on the ship's bow for the next thirty years.

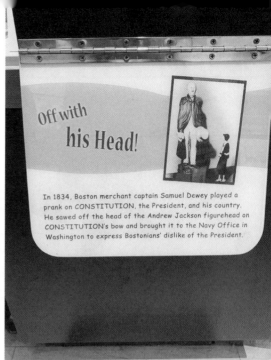

You learn the story of how Andrew Jackson's figurehead was sawed off the USS Constitution *in 1834 at the museum.*

Dewey wasn't able to saw off the whole head because of a large iron bolt within the figure's neck, so he cut it off just below the nose. A portion of the lower part of the wooden head, long assumed to be missing, was positively identified in 2010 on the PBS program *History Detectives*. Today, the original fragment is displayed below a plaster cast of the rest of the head at the museum.

9/11 TRIBUTE

Where can you see a monument to the passengers and crew who left from Logan Airport on 9/11?

On September 11, 2001, America and the world were changed forever by unspeakable acts of terrorism. Unfortunately, Logan Airport was the departure point for American Airlines Flight 11 and United Airlines Flight 175, two planes that were headed for Los Angeles but were hijacked by terrorists who flew them into the World Trade Center towers in New York.

The Logan Airport 9/11 Memorial is a permanent memorial that honors the passengers and crews of both flights. Designed by Moskow Linn Architects of Boston, *The Place of Remembrance* was chosen by a public design competition that was judged by a committee of local stakeholders, including representatives from the two airlines, design professionals, Massachusetts Port Authority officials, and the families of those lost in the attacks. It is located next to the Hilton Boston Logan Airport because the hotel was a base for the family assistance program after the tragedy.

The memorial is a large, cube-shaped glass pavilion that visitors can enter from paths representing each flight. Inside, the two flights are memorialized by glass panels—one side of each panel is etched with the names of every person aboard the

There's another memorial to the victims: two American flags flying above the jetway at the gates where the flights departed. The flag above gate B-32 honors the crew and passengers of American Airlines Flight 11, and the flag above gate C-19 is for those who died on United Airlines Flight 175.

A poignant remembrance to 9/11 victims is located near Logan Airport.

flight, and the other side simply states the time the flight departed the airport. From inside the cube, you can look up at a prism of reflective panels that change with the sunlight. In the evening, the cube is softly lit from within.

While the memorial is a sad reminder of loss, it is also meant to be a place of peace for friends, family, and the Logan Airport community.

LOGAN AIRPORT 9/11 MEMORIAL

WHAT Tribute to lives lost

WHERE 1 Hotel Dr.

COST Free

PRO TIP The memorial is a bit tricky to find. Look for it outside the Hilton Boston Logan Airport.

SHIPS IN THE NIGHT

What's the story with the big red ship in East Boston with the word "Nantucket" painted on it?

The largest lightship ever built in the United States happens to be docked in East Boston. Now a museum, Nantucket Lightship/ *LV-112* guided transoceanic shipping to and from East Coast ports for thirty-nine years. The vessel, manned by members of the US Coast Guard, was stationed one hundred miles offshore from the Massachusetts coast. Its imposing foghorn and beacon worked to guide ships through the perilously shallow Nantucket Shoals, which claimed many a ship over the years.

Now a National Historic Landmark, the *LV-112* is the world's most famous US lightship. She was the first symbol of America many thousands of immigrants saw as they approached the United States from the sea and was the last lightship seen by departing vessels. Ships such as the SS *United States*, the *Queen Mary*, the *Normandie*, and naval cargo vessels depended on *LV-112* as a navigational aid.

Built in 1936 in Wilmington, Delaware, the vessel was actually paid for by the White Star Line as compensation for the 1934 collision and sinking of *LV-112*'s predecessor, *LV-117*. That ship was on duty at the Nantucket Station when it was rammed by the RMS *Olympic*, the sister ship to the *Titanic*. Seven of the lightship's eleven crew members were killed.

Between 1820 and 1952, 179 lightships were built. At one time, fifty-one lightships were stationed around the United States (forty-six on the Eastern Seaboard and five on the Pacific Coast). Today, only seventeen lightships still exist.

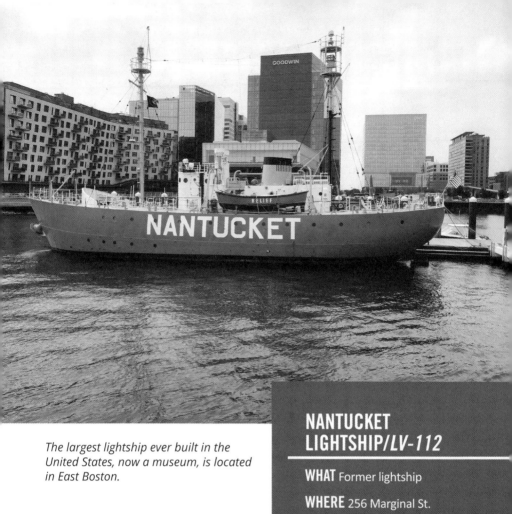

The largest lightship ever built in the United States, now a museum, is located in East Boston.

NANTUCKET LIGHTSHIP/*LV-112*

WHAT Former lightship

WHERE 256 Marginal St.

COST $8 donation

PRO TIP The ship is open from the last Saturday in April through the last Saturday in October from 10 a.m. to 4 p.m.

There was no chance of that happening again. *LV-112* was built to the specifications of a wartime US Navy vessel, with a double hull and a high degree of compartmentalization, making it virtually unsinkable.

During World War II, *LV-112* was taken off duty as a lightship and designated the USS *Nantucket*. Painted battleship gray, she functioned as an examination patrol vessel off the coast of Portland, Maine, and rescued crewmembers of the USS *Eagle 56*, a patrol boat that was torpedoed and sunk by German U-boat *U-853*. (The *U-853* was later tracked down and sunk by the US Navy in Rhode Island waters, where it lies submerged to this day.)

ROOM TO GROW

Where did the Institute of Contemporary Art open a new gallery?

Boston's Institute of Contemporary Art can always be counted on for its cutting-edge art, with ever-changing exhibitions, plus live music and dance performances, film, lectures, tours, and more. One of its latest and greatest projects is the ICA Watershed, which opened in the Boston Harbor Shipyard and Marina in East Boston in the summer of 2018.

The Watershed is located in a fifteen-thousand-square-foot building, once a copper pipe facility that had been condemned. The museum turned it into an enormous open space, enabling the nonprofit to expand its artistic footprint. Each year, the ICA invites one artist to create a site-specific work or installation for the summer season.

On permanent display at the Watershed is a gallery detailing the history of the shipyard and East Boston, with an overview of the area's development. A map shows what it looked like in the early 1800s and features the group of five islands that once comprised East Boston. A video presents historians, community leaders, and residents who talk about the neighborhood's evolution over the years.

While you can drive to the Watershed, it's much more fun to take a water taxi from the dock by the ICA. You get to enjoy the views and see a different perspective of the area.

The Watershed is only open from about May to September, but there is still plenty of art to enjoy all around the waterfront, including in Piers Park by the dock.

The Institute of Contemporary Art's newest space is across the harbor.

ICA WATERSHED

WHAT Satellite ICA space

WHERE 256 Marginal St.

COST Admission to the Watershed is free.

PRO TIP If you purchase admission to the ICA, roundtrip water shuttle transportation between the Watershed and the ICA is included.

HOLY MOTHER OF MARY

Why is there a giant statue of Mary perched atop the globe in East Boston?

Located on a hilltop in Orient Heights, accessed by a series of winding roads in East Boston, stands an unexpected sight—a giant statue of Mary, the mother of Jesus, standing on a sphere. It is as surprising to suddenly come upon as it is undeniably impressive. The sculpture stands within immense granite pillars that are capped by a gold crown.

The thirty-foot-tall bronze-and-copper Madonna Queen of the Universe shrine was erected in 1954 at the national headquarters of the Don Orione order. The work of Jewish-Italian sculptor Arrigo Minerbi, the statue is a full-size replica of his original Madonna overlooking Rome. How this Jewish sculptor came to craft works for the Catholic Church is a moving story.

Prior to World War II, Arrigo Minerbi had worked as a successful artist in Italy. To escape persecution during the 1940 invasion of Italy by Nazi forces, Minerbi went into hiding with help from the Roman Catholic priests of the Don Orione order of Rome.

In 1953, a grateful Minerbi designed a monumental statue of Mary that was erected at the order's center in Rome. When the order opened a home for the elderly in East Boston's Orient Heights, Minerbi oversaw the casting of the six-ton bronze-and-copper replica in Italy. The statue was then shipped to Boston in three pieces and reconstructed. It was dedicated as *The Madonna Queen of the Universe* by then-Archbishop Richard Cushing in 1954.

The shrine's plaza sits atop a church and offers sweeping panoramic views of Logan Airport and the Boston skyline. It is a spectacular place to see sunsets.

Head to East Boston to see the stunning
35-foot-tall bronze and copper Madonna
Queen of the Universe *statue, erected
in 1954, located on the national
headquarters of the Order of Don Orione.*

MADONNA QUEEN OF THE UNIVERSE SHRINE

WHAT Unique statue

WHERE 150 Orient Ave.

COST Free

PRO TIP The statue was first
placed over the Don Orione
Nursing Home, but it was later
moved across the street to its
current home on a large plaza.

MOVING HOUSE

Did a rich Detroit businessman have his entire mansion moved piece by piece from Michigan to Massachusetts?

The Longyear Museum, located in Chestnut Hill, is dedicated to advancing the understanding of the life and work of Mary Baker Eddy, the founder and leader of Christian Science. It features documents, artifacts, photos, and exhibits about Eddy and the people who helped her. And while that story is fascinating, the building itself has its own amazing story.

Michigan native John Munro Longyear made a fortune developing lumber and mineral resources in the Northwest, and in 1890 he commissioned the construction of a home befitting that fortune overlooking Lake Superior in Marquette. By the mid-1890s, however, the railroad obtained right of way through the Longyear property, ruining much of its value. And so, as one does, Longyear decided to move the entire house somewhere more scenic. In the end, the Longyears relocated the house—and themselves—to Brookline.

Starting in January 1903, the house was dismantled, with each block of stone carefully wrapped and numbered. The pieces were sent to Brookline on two freight trains totaling 190 cars. Almost everything arrived intact, and windows, doors, and many structural units were reused. But that doesn't mean the house was rebuilt in exactly the same way. The old house had sixty-four rooms, while the new one had almost one hundred. The kitchen

When the Longyear house was completed and the family moved in on March 25, 1906, it had about 50 percent more space than the original house.

The Longyear Museum was formerly a home, which was moved from Michigan, piece by piece.

LONGYEAR MUSEUM

WHAT Relocated house

WHERE 1125 Boylston St.

COST Free

PRO TIP The museum is open Monday, Thursday, Friday, and Saturday from 10 a.m. to 4 p.m. and on Sundays from 1 to 4 p.m.

was moved from the basement to the first floor, a large bowling alley was installed, and a music room and sun porch were added. The family finally moved into the house in 1906.

John's wife, Mary Beecher Longyear (1851–1931), was introduced to Christian Science in the 1880s and became a devoted member. She established the Longyear Foundation in 1923, and the Longyear Museum opened to the public in 1937.

A FUTURE KING SLEPT HERE

Who is the first monarch to be born in the United States?

An easy-to-miss plaque on an apartment building in Brookline reveals an interesting fact: a future king of Thailand once lived there. King Bhumibol Adulyadej was born in 1927 at Mount Auburn Hospital in Cambridge. His father, Prince Mahidol of Siam (Thailand), had come to the United States in 1916 to study public health at Harvard.

The prince met his wife, who was a Thai student studying nursing at Simmons College, while in Massachusetts. The couple moved back to Thailand but returned in 1926 so Prince Mahidol could attend Harvard Medical School.

Their third child, the future king, was born the following year, and the family moved to 63 Longwood Avenue in Brookline, where they lived until 1928. King Adulyadej, also called King Rama IX, ascended to the throne in 1946 and reigned for seventy years. He passed away in 2016 at age eighty-eight.

The plaque exists thanks to the King of Thailand Birthplace Foundation, a nonprofit organization incorporated in 1998. Its mission is to preserve Thai history throughout the state of Massachusetts. They've installed more than eleven historic sites in Massachusetts and two sites in New Hampshire.

Massachusetts is an important place in Thailand's history, so much so that there is a Trail of Thai Royalty that traces the king's family during their time here. It marks their lives, homes, and places where the family stayed from 1916 to 1928.

A plaque marks where King Bhumibol Adulyadej of Thailand, the first monarch to be born in the US was born.

BIRTHPLACE OF THAI KING

WHAT First steps to monarchy

WHERE 63 Longwood Ave., Brookline

COST Free

PRO TIP A Harvard Square monument, located at Eliot and Bennett Streets, marks the Massachusetts history of King Bhumibol.

TEEN HERO

Was this Brookline teenager the youngest American soldier in World War I?

Albert Edward Scott, a Brookline newsboy whose nickname was "Scotty," was just fifteen years old when he lied to a recruiter about his age and enlisted as a private to fight in World War I. The high school freshman would become famous in his death, which happened only a year into his service.

Scott was serving as a rifleman with the infantry in France when he was ordered—alone—to guard the exposed rear flank of his company as it made its way along the roads of Trugity Woods. According to *Boston Globe* news reports from 1918, Scott reportedly killed or injured thirty or so German soldiers before he was drawn out of his position, reportedly by an American fighting with the Germans, and killed by a sniper. He was discovered by his fellow soldiers slumped over his machine gun, surrounded by the bodies of fallen enemy soldiers.

An August 29, 1918, a newspaper account in the *Boston Globe* starkly reported, "Private Scott was only 16 years old. He was shot through the head by the Germans after he killed 30 of the enemy."

His story was widely recounted in papers across the country, and Scott became a hero. A group called the Roosevelt Newsboys' Association of Boston raised $2,000 to erect a bronze plaque memorializing his final moments. The plaque

TRIBUTE TO YOUNG HERO

WHAT War memorial

WHERE Babcock and Freeman Sts., Brookline

COST Free

PRO TIP In 2018, one hundred years after Scott's death, he was posthumously awarded an honorary Brookline High School diploma during Veterans Day ceremonies.

Allegedly the youngest American soldier to serve in World War I was born in Brookline. This plaque shows the last moments of 16-year-old Albert Edward Scott.

is modeled after a painting by artist Gale Hoskins and shows Scott's death at a crossroads in the woods. The memorial was dedicated on October 29, 1921.

The ceremony was a big deal. William Jennings Bryan, former secretary of state and the Democratic presidential nominee, spoke at the dedication. The Boston School Committee gave newsboys the afternoon off to attend the ceremony and the Boston Elevated kicked in free transport for all newsboys to get to the ceremony and back home with their newsboy badges.

The newsboy plaque sits outside Brookline Town Hall, on the back side of a memorial to fallen soldiers from every war since World War I.

PAPER TRAIL

Is the largest collection of handmade toilet paper in the world located here?

From the street, the one-hundred-year-old-plus building, originally used as a carriage house, looks like one more historic property in Brookline. Inside, however, it's a different story. The ground floor houses a working hand papermaking studio, complete with plants used to make paper, while upstairs a museum dedicated to the craft is packed with displays.

Elaine Koretsky, who became interested in papermaking in 1970, founded the nonprofit Research Institute of Paper History & Technology in 1994. She is the author of several books, articles, and films on the subject. Over the years, while traveling the world on expeditions to mills and villages devoted to hand papermaking, Koretsky amassed an enormous collection of rare books, handmade paper, and artifacts used in the making of paper, many on display in the institute's International Paper Museum.

One highlight of the museum is a collection of rare accordion-folded prayer books from Southeast Asia, the most exceptional of which is a sixteenth-century manuscript from the Khmer era in Cambodia that is illuminated by palace paintings. Other standouts include books made of palm leaves into which the writing is incised; lacquer manuscripts; and other examples of ancient writings on media as varied as amatl, papyrus, vellum, and metal.

Going to New York any time soon? Koretsky's daughter cofounded Carriage House Paper in Brooklyn, a teaching studio and papermaking facility open to the public.

Check out the collection of rare books, handmade paper and artifacts used in the making of paper at the International Paper Museum in Brookline.

A quirkier part of the collection is the handmade toilet paper exhibit from China, Vietnam, and Myanmar, which the museum thinks might be the largest in the world. China, where paper was invented, is said to be the first to make paper for sanitary purposes, at least as early as the ninth century AD.

STAR SEARCH

Where can you observe the stars with professional equipment?

You'd probably never know about the Clay Center Observatory in Brookline unless you're an astronomy fan, an amateur radio operator, or affiliated somehow with the Dexter Southfield School.

The observatory, operated by the private K–12 educational institution, is located at the top of the five-story Clay Center for Science & Technology, a state-of-the-art learning facility. It's equipped with a custom-made Ritchey-Chrétien reflecting telescope, similar in optical design to the Hubble Space Telescope.

There are several opportunities over the course of the year to visit the facility. In the spring and fall on Tuesday nights, if the weather cooperates, the observatory is open for public telescope viewing. Besides seeing planets, the moon, and stars, there's a great view of Boston from the observation decks.

Exhibits at the center include the Sun Court, a scale-model of the planets and orbits of the inner solar system; the Moon Court, where you can observe lunar phases from full moon to new moon on surrounding brass globes; and the Stars Court, which illustrates classical constellation figures of the northern sky.

The biggest event at the observatory is held on National Astronomy Day in the spring, with science exhibits, demonstrations, planetarium shows, laser light shows, rocketry,

CLAY CENTER OBSERVATORY

WHAT Observe the night sky

WHERE 20 Newton Street, Brookline

COST Free

PRO TIP Visitors need to call to register in advance at 617-751-3409.

The Clay Center Observatory in Brookline offers a way for the public to stargaze. Photo courtesy of Clay Center Observatory.

stunt kites, and hands-on educational activities. Several different telescopes are set up to use, both to view the sun in the daytime and to see planets and stars in the evening.

The observatory often opens the roof deck and puts out smaller telescopes that you can control, and an astronomer is on hand to point out constellations and other naked-eye objects.

CRAZY FOR CARS

Where can you see the oldest automobile collection in the United States?

In late 1800s and early 1900s, wealthy socialites Larz and Isabel Anderson, who lived in Brookline (among other places), picked up quite a hobby: buying cars. In fact, they bought a car almost every year from 1899 to 1948. Their first one was an 1899 Winton Runabout, basically a horseless carriage. In total, they would acquire thirty-two brand-new automobiles over the course of their lives.

The Andersons kept their cars at their Brookline estate in a castle-like carriage house, built in 1888 and designed by Edmund M. Wheelwright, the city architect of Boston. It was constructed to stable horses, but it later came to house the car collection. The beautiful building is on the National Register of Historic Places. After Isabel's death in 1948 (Larz passed away in 1937), at her direction, it was turned into a museum.

Today, visitors can see fourteen of their cars, including their very first purchase, at the museum. Probably their most famous—and most expensive—car purchase on display is a 1906 Charron-Girodot-Voigt. They picked it up while vacationing in France and nicknamed it the "Winniepocket," after the couple's vacation home in New Hampshire.

The car is delightfully quirky, with all sorts of cool gadgets and upgrades. The rear seat converted into a bed, and under two smaller seats were a wash bin and a toilet. Isabel installed a tiny drawing room for herself as well. The Andersons had a

This museum hosts car shows on the lawn from May to October, with cars from both the estate and other collections.

Top: *Even the Carriage House at the Larz Anderson Auto Museum is a stunner.*

Bottom: *One of the gems of the collection at the Larz Anderson Auto Museum is the 1906 Charron-Girodot-Voight. Photo courtesy of the Larz Anderson Auto Museum.*

LARZ ANDERSON AUTO MUSEUM

WHAT America's oldest car collection

WHERE Goddard Ave. and Newton St., Brookline

COST $10

PRO TIP Isabel Anderson was the first woman in Massachusetts to obtain a driver's license.

chauffeur to drive them longer distances in the car, such as to Washington, DC, where they had another house.

The museum is located in Larz Anderson Park, which also features a pond, acres of open space with walking paths, and a seasonal outdoor ice-skating rink.

FINE-FEATHERED FRIENDS

Where can you find a park once owned by one of the founders of the Massachusetts Audubon Society?

Hall's Pond Sanctuary and Amory Woods make up a five-acre gem of protected space improbably located in busy Brookline. What many people might not know is that the pond used to be called Swallow Pond, and it was owned in 1850 by the family of Minna Hall. Minna and her cousin, Harriet Hemenway, organized meetings that led to the founding of the Massachusetts Audubon Society in 1896.

Hemenway and Hall, outraged at the killing of wading birds whose feathers were commonly used at that time to decorate ladies' hats, were determined to protect their feathered friends. They enlisted their fellow Brahmin society ladies to boycott the trade. They also asked noted ornithologist William Brewster to serve as the Massachusetts Audubon Society's first president (1896–1913) to advance legislation to restrict the killing of birds and sale of their plumage. The savvy women knew a male president was needed for the organization to be taken seriously at the time.

In 1918 President Wilson signed the Migratory Bird Treaty Act, which remains to this day one of the strongest laws protecting wild North American birds.

Today, the town-owned property is one of just two natural ponds left in Brookline, and the sanctuary is a bird and animal paradise. Great blue herons, black-crowned night herons,

By 1898 state-level Audubon Societies had been established in Pennsylvania, New York, New Hampshire, Illinois, Maine, and ten other states. In 1905 the National Association of Audubon Societies was incorporated in New York State.

Hall's Pond Sanctuary and Amory Woods, a 5-acre green space in Brookline, used to be owned by the family of Minna Hall, one of the founders of the Massachusetts Audubon Society. Photo courtesy of Jorge Abellas-Martin.

HALL'S POND

WHAT Hidden garden

WHERE Amory and Freeman streets

COST Free

PRO TIP The park is open from dawn to dusk.

kingfishers, and red-winged blackbirds are just a few of the species who visit, making it a birder's paradise and a fitting tribute to its former owner and champion.

HOME OFFICE

Where did Frederick Law Olmsted set up the world's first professional office for the practice of landscape design?

Frederick Law Olmsted's creations, from the parks in Boston's Emerald Necklace to Central Park in New York City, are well known, but Fairsted in Brookline flies a bit under the radar. The property, now a National Historic Site, is where, in 1883, Olmsted opened the first professional office in the world fully devoted to landscape design. From this spot, Olmsted, his sons, and their associates designed thousands of landscapes across North America.

The original eighteen-room farmhouse, which dates to 1810, was renovated by Olmsted, who increased it by another eighteen rooms, many of which you can tour. Don't miss the 1904 "electric blueprint machine," a kind of primitive photocopier that takes up part of an entire room. During the next century, his sons and successors kept to his design ideals and philosophy. Olmsted's office even played an influential role in the creation of the National Park Service, which now cares for the property.

But, fittingly, what is probably most interesting are the grounds. At less than two acres, they are sort of a mini-snapshot of Olmsted's designs and a charming way to while away an afternoon. The Hollow, a sunken garden, looks like it was designed by fairies. You descend carved Roxbury "puddingstone" steps into a green landscape and follow a path

Ranger-guided tours are offered at 10 a.m., 11 a.m., 1 p.m., 2 p.m., and 3 p.m. The Design Office can only be viewed by guided tour, but the grounds are open from dawn to dusk.

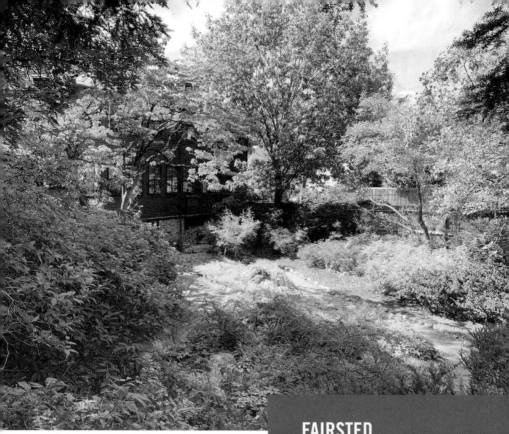

Frederick Law Olmsted's home and office, called Fairsted, was the world's first full-scale professional office for the practice of landscape design.

around in a circle. On the other side of the property, visitors can take a short and shady walk through the Rock Garden, which suddenly opens onto a large green lawn.

FAIRSTED

WHAT Olmsted's home and landscape office

WHERE 99 Warren St., Brookline

COST Free

PRO TIP The house is open seasonally from April through December.

GLOVE LOVE

What is the meaning of the random-looking bronze gloves scattered about the subway?

Located in the Porter Square subway station, placed seemingly willy-nilly next to the subway's long escalator and elsewhere in the station, are dozens of life-size bronze gloves scattered around looking lost or abandoned. They certainly make a commuter pause and look again.

The somewhat unusual installation was created by local artist Mags Harries, who also created another popular installation located at Haymarket (see page 108). On her website, she describes a trip through the subway station as a daily ritual for people, one designed to move commuters along a certain path as efficiently as possible. On this path there are places where the commuter pauses along the way, such as the escalator or the platform.

According to Harries, the positioning of the cast-bronze gloves echoes this pattern, to make a sculptural narrative. It begins at the token booth and ends on the train platform, creating a subway life cycle. The separate gloves that you see throughout the station add up to not just a life cycle of the glove but also a whimsical metaphor for the journey of life to death.

And since we're in Boston, the gloves also are a fitting monument to the pains of winter. What commuter hasn't lost a glove or scarf or hat in the rush of trying to catch a train? Perhaps one of the gloves resembles one you lost, and now you can imagine it is forever enshrined.

Head to Haymarket to see *Asaroton*, where Harries's embedded bronze pieces replicate the trash and debris that might normally cover the street.

The Glove Cycle *is an intriguing large art installation in the Porter Square Subway Station. Photos by Will Burnett.*

GLOVE CYCLE

WHAT Public art

WHERE Porter Square subway station

COST Free

PRO TIP There are fifty-four gloves in the piece.

HUNGER GAME

Do people really line up for the chance to buy a burger?

When a burger makes the cover of *Bon Appétit* magazine, it's worth looking into. Craigie on Main, located in Cambridge, is where James Beard Award-winning chef and owner Tony Maws whips up his signature burger. To be more precise, the burger, which has garnered international fame, is actually only available in the bar, COMB (short for Craigie on Main Bar), and only eighteen are made each night.

The iconic burger, which often sells out in minutes, is composed of locally sourced, grass-fed beef (a magical blend of brisket, short ribs, hanger steak, bone marrow, and suet), sprinkled with miso, and topped with Shelburne cheddar, house-made pickles, and mace ketchup, all served on a milk bun with steak fries on the side.

Either you get it or you don't—some people can't fathom the hype—but since the burger has been a staple for more than a decade and is sold out nightly, more people apparently get it than not. As far as I'm concerned, it's totally worth the wait and the splurge.

No need to be depressed if you miss out, though. There are plenty of other delectable items on the bar menu to sample, like the crispy-fried heritage pork ribs or heritage pork rillettes.

CRAIGIE BURGER

WHAT Limited-availability burger

WHERE 853 Main St., Cambridge

COST $26

PRO TIP If you want the burger, line up early.

You have to line up early to get your hands on one these limited burgers at Craigie on Main. Photo by Michael Piazza.

Don't want to wait in line and take the chance of missing out? Head to Time Out Boston Market in Fenway instead, where a very similar burger can be had at Craigie Burger, with no limits!

SWEET DREAMS

Where is there a nod to a thin wafer candy?

Easy to miss, a tiny sculpture on a boulder in the corner of a Cambridge park pays homage to the humble candy and what was the oldest operating candy company in the United States, the New England Confectionery Company (NECCO). Its factory was once located near the park where the sculpture is found.

The Necco Wafer Memorial Sculpture, which depicts metal NECCO wafers spilling out of a bag, is the work of artist Ross Miller. It was installed as part of the construction of University Park at MIT in 1998. After 171 years, in 2018, the company went bust, much to the horror of its fans, but there is hope another company will bring its confections back.

While the wafers may have tasted more like sweet chalk than candy (in eight flavors: chocolate, licorice, cinnamon, lemon, lime, orange, wintergreen, and clove), they stood the test of time—invented in 1847, they became an unlikely American icon. Explorers took them to the Arctic and the South Pole, and the US government even made them part of the rations for soldiers in World War II.

The candy was the brainchild of Oliver Chase of Boston, after he invented and patented the first candy machine in 1847 to cut wafers, which he called "hub wafers." After a couple of mergers and partnerships, NECCO was born in 1901. Over the years, the company prospered and invented many other well-known products, such as Squirrel Nut Zippers, Clark Bars, and Sky Bars.

Miss the candy? Keep your figures crossed. The Spangler Candy Company is said to be relaunching the popular candy, with the exact recipe, sometime in 2019.

This sculpture honors a long-beloved candy, the NECCO wafer, which used to be produced locally. After 171 years, in 2018, the company went bust. Photo courtesy of Sadie MacKinnon

NECCO WAFER MEMORIAL SCULPTURE

WHAT Public art

WHERE 108 Franklin St., University Park, Cambridge

COST Free

PRO TIP Look closely and you'll see some conversation hearts mixed in the bag too.

The original NECCO factory was located in South Boston, then moved to Cambridge, first near the MIT campus on Massachusetts Avenue and then to Lechmere Square. In 2003 the company relocated for the last time to a factory in Revere.

A plaque on the side of the boulder on which the sculpture sits reads in part: "Necco SWEETS are the kind that hurt no one; the kind everybody—old and young—wants in preference to others; the kind you can't forget, because of their goodness."

URBAN OASIS

Where can you find a peaceful park in an unlikely location?

Normally, no one thinks of a parking garage as a great place to hang out, but Kendall Square has one that is definitely a destination to check out. Or, rather, its roof is. On top of the six-story Green Garage, visitors are delighted to find the Kendall Square Roof Garden, a not-so-secret garden surrounded by buildings.

This beautifully landscaped space features flowers and flower beds, a variety of trees, rose bushes, winding paths, grassy patches, benches, picnic tables, and a lovely view of the Boston skyline. People come to get a breath of fresh air, smell the flowers, eat lunch, birdwatch, or simply relax.

Green City Growers hosts urban garden programs on the roof, including cooking demos and tips, and the produce grown in the community gardens is donated to a local food bank. There are also occasional fitness classes offered on the roof. It really is an outdoor public space embraced and used to the fullest by locals, but it offers everyone a place to enjoy the outdoors in peace.

Just outside the parking garage is Kendall Plaza, which is home to a seasonal farmer's market, a concert series, and other free public events.

Tech-heavy Kendall Center, where the park is located, is home to businesses like Akamai Technologies, Biogen, Google, Microsoft, MIT, Novartis, and The Broad Institute.

This rooftop garden is a city oasis with great views. Photo by Will Burnett.

KENDALL SQUARE ROOFTOP GARDEN

WHAT Rooftop garden

WHERE 325 Main St., Cambridge

COST Free

PRO TIP The park is open daily from dawn to dusk.

GLAD RAGS

Where is there an endless treasure trove of new and used clothes?

For anyone who loves shopping and the thrill of finding the perfect piece of clothing amid thousands of cast-offs, the Garment District is the place for you. The enormous twelve-thousand-square-foot "alternative" retail store, located in Cambridge, offers both new and used women's, men's, and children's clothes, shoes, and accessories. Every day, new items are put out, so you rarely see the same things twice.

What makes the Garment District beloved by frugal shoppers, college students, and thrift-shop fans is its wild practice of selling clothes by the pound. Every morning when the store opens, an 850-pound bale of clothing is cut open and simply plopped on the floor in a giant pile. On the weekends, several bales are opened. Shoppers wade into the mishmash of mixed-up clothes, which run the gamut of decades, styles, and sizes, to see what they can find. Then they are charged two dollars a pound for their picks.

How this practice and the store came to be is a fun story. In 1981 Harbor Textile, which manufactured and sold wiping cloths and gloves, put out a few bales of clothing every Saturday for the public to browse through and buy by the pound. It was a huge hit. In 1986 the Garment District opened as an off-shoot, and over the years, it's grown into the phenomenon that it is today. In 2007 it was joined by Boston Costume, which has been in business since 1965.

GARMENT DISTRICT

WHAT Discounted clothing

WHERE 200 Broadway, Cambridge

COST Varies

PRO TIP On Fridays, Pay by the Pound is half-price, at just one dollar a pound.

The Garment District is a great place to find used and new clothes, with an unusual pay-by-the-pound section. Photos by Sadie MacKinnon.

The Garment District's building is the last standing structure associated with the city's once-booming soap manufacturing industry, dating back to 1893. Until World War II, the building housed soap manufacturer Lysander Kemp & Sons.

THIS OLD HOUSE, PART II

Where is the oldest remaining timber-frame home in the country located?

There's no doubt that Boston is filled with historic homes and landmarks, but the oldest remaining timber-frame home in the country is actually not in the city—it's located just outside, in Dedham. While other buildings of this type were constructed earlier, the Fairbanks House is the oldest known to still survive today.

Constructed between 1637 and 1641, the Fairbanks House was built for a family of Puritan immigrants from Yorkshire, England. Jonathan and Grace Fairebanke lived there with their six children, and the house ended up being home to eight generations of the family. Even now, although it's a museum, it's still family owned and run by the Fairbanks Family in America, Inc., a genealogical membership organization made up of descendants of Jonathan and Grace.

The last family member to live in the house moved out in 1904, and that's when it was turned into a museum. The original house had four rooms surrounding a massive center chimney—two on the first floor and two on the second, with an attic above that. Later owners made several additions, including the current west and east wings, the privy off the lean-to (originally a dairy) and the mud room entrance. The decision was made not to attempt to restore the house to

One of the museum's most prized possessions was lost for decades. The Fairbanks Chest, carved circa 1652–1665, was a fixture in the house through the late nineteenth century, when it was sold. In 2003 the museum managed to buy it back in an auction.

The oldest remaining timber-frame home in the country, now a museum, was constructed between 1637 and 1641 and is still remains in the hands of the same family.

FAIRBANKS HOUSE

WHAT One family's legacy

WHERE 511 East St., Dedham

COST $12

PRO TIP The house is open for tours only from May through October.

its appearance at any one period of time, so it provides detailed evidence of the many different time periods of its construction and use.

SOURCES

1. **Dressed Up Ducks:** In-person site visit. schon.com/
public/ducklings-boston.php
2. **Can't Believe Your Eyes:** In-person site visit.
bostonmagazine.com/property/2018/04/18/scarlett-
ohara-house-beacon-hill
3. **Death Notice:** Interview with Maria Daniels, Director
of Communications and Patron Services, Boston
Athenæum. bostonathenaeum.org
4. **Take a Deep Breath:** In-person site visit. massgeneral.
org/museum/exhibits/etherdome
5. **Phone Home:** In-person site visit. britannica.com/
biography/Alexander-Graham-Bell; bostonglobe.com/
metro/2019/02/12/years-ago-globe-and-alexander-
graham-bell-made-history/eps7LNZk245BoBNykVO5EJ/
story.html
6. **A Head Case, Among Other Things:** In-person site
visit. countway.harvard.edu/center-history-medicine/
warren-anatomical-museum
7. **Movie Magic:** In-person site visit
8. **Trailblazers:** In-person site visit. maah.org/boston_
heritage_trail
9. **Weather Report:** In-person site visit. Charlie Pigott,
Dylan Freitas, Thomas Lefavor, "Old John Hancock
Building," *Boston History*, accessed July 30, 2019,
explorebostonhistory.org/items/show/18. worldatlas.
com/articles/tallest-buildings-in-boston.html
10. **Tea Time:** In-person site visit
11. **Time Capsules:** In-person site visit. mos.org/history
12. **Writer's Blocks:** In-person site visit. thefreedomtrail.
org/about/freedom-trail-establishment
13. **Return Appearance:** In-person site visit. bostonpoe.org;
eapoe.org/works/letters/p4902140.htm

14. **Table Talk:** In-person site visit. *Heaven, By Hotel Standards: The History of the Omni Parker House* by Susan Wilson. masshist.org/collection-guides/view/fa0358; omnihotels.com/hotels/boston-parker-house/property-details/history

15. **Tuneful Teddy:** In-person sightings. keytarbear.com; trilliumbrewing.com/keytar-bear-double-ipa

16. **Hit the Highway:** In-person site visit. mass.gov/info-details/the-big-dig-project-background

17. **Name Game:** In-person site visit

18. **Not So Secret:** In-person site visit. massfreemasonry.org/boston-masonic-building

19. **Love at First Sight:** In-person site visit. bostonpreservation.org/news-item/roger-webb-and-democratic-donkey

20. **Trendsetter:** In-person site visit. oldcityhall.com/today

21. **Hot Pot:** In-person site visit. theclio.com/entry/61135. *Boston Globe* newspaper archives, January 1 and 2, 1875

22. **Rock On:** In-person site visit. waymarking.com/waymarks/WMD800_The_Boston_Stone_Boston_MA

23. **Bottoms Up:** In-person site visit. mrbostondrinks.com/recipes/ward-eight; yvonnesboston.com

24. **Lost to Time:** In-person site visit. pialleygarage.com/pub/history; bostonglobe.com/metro/2018/07/19/one-city-oldest-byways-frozen-time

25. **Politics as Usual:** In-person site visit. boston.com/news/local-news/2016/02/11/tbt-when-massachusetts-coined-the-term-gerrymandering

26. **Special Request:** Interview with Josh Kantor

27. **Another Brick in the . . . Ground:** In-person site visit. katekburke.com/section/143743-Boston-Bricks.html

28. **Underground Art:** In-person site visit. undergroundinkblock.com/about-2

29. **True Colors:** Paint purchase.

30. **Unbrotherly Love:** In-person site visit. bostonmagazine. com/property/2017/03/31/north-end-skinny-house-for-sale

31. **Sticky Flood of Destruction:** In-person site visit to plaque. history.com/news/the-great-molasses-flood-of-1919. Dark Tide: The Great Boston Molasses Flood of 1919 by Stephen Puleo.

32. **Model Citizen:** In-person site visit. friendsnorthendlibrary.blogspot.com/p/blog-page_6. html

33. **Labor of Love:** In-person site visit. wgbh.org/ news/2017/05/25/how-we-live/north-end-changes-all-saints-way-abides

34. **Follow Your Nose:** In-person site visit. briccosalumeria. com/panetteria

35. **Anthony! Anthony!:** In-person site visit. youtube.com/ watch?time_continue=60&v=P8ti1hnLiLw; princepasta. com/en-us/content/27448/OurStory.aspx

36. **Beloved Billboard:** In-person viewing. boston.gov/ sites/default/files/imce-uploads/2018-09/citgo_sign_ subcommittee_final_draft.pdf

37. **Long Live the Rat!:** In-person site visit. hotelcommonwealth.com/accommodations/signature-suites

38. **Bold as Brass:** In-person site visit. gardnermuseum.org/ organization/theft

39. **Secret Garden:** In-person site visit. mfa.org/collections/ featured-galleries/japanese-garden-tenshin-en

40. **Retro Rock-and-Roll Dream:** In-person site visit. theverbhotel.com

41. **He Measured Up:** In-person site visit. technologyreview. com/s/410360/smoots-legacy

42. **Master Promoter:** In-person site visit to plaque. *Boston Globe*, "Overboard Chained, Houdini Gets Free," May 1, 1908; *Boston Globe*, "Houdini Escapes from Big Turtle," September 27, 1911

43. **Whalespotting:** In-person site visit. dzlart.com/Murals-Businesses.html

44. **Shape-Shifter:** In-person site visit. armenianheritagepark.org

45. **What Lies Beneath:** In-person site visit. harriesheder.com/project/asaroton

46. **Reuse, Recycle, Recreate, Part I:** In-person site visit. bostonharborislands.org/spectacle-island

47. **Lighting the Way:** In-person site visit. nps.gov/boha/learn/historyculture/boston-light.htm

48. **A Rescue Gone Awry:** In-person site visit. bostonharborislands.org/georges-island

49. **Bird's-Eye View:** In-person site visit. marriott.com/hotels/hotel-photos/bosch-marriott-vacation-club-pulse-at-custom-house-boston

50. **Dairy King:** In-person site visit. bostonchildrensmuseum.wordpress.com/2015/12/21/that-giant-milk-bottle

51. **Aerosmith Slept Here:** In-person site visit. wbur.org/news/2012/11/05/aerosmith-boston-concert; rockhall.com/inductees/aerosmith

52. **The Play's the Thing:** In-person site visit. footlight.org; jphs.org/victorian-era/the-footlight-club-at-125-years.html

53. **Can't Sit Here:** In-person site visit. massart.edu/faculty/matthew-hincman

54. **Tiny Houses:** In-person site visit. christopherfrost.org/#/neighbors2006

55. **On the Flip Side:** In-person site visit. tresgatosjp.com

56. **Bonsai Bonanza:** In-person site visit. arboretum.harvard.edu/plants/featured-plants/bonsai

57. **All Aboard:** In-person site visit. bsmrm.org

58. **Train Wreck:** In-person site visit; roslindalehistoricalsociety.org/Images/NYTimes.pdf; bostonglobe.newspapers.com/image/430875670/?term s=bussey%2Bbridge%2Btrain.

59. **Reuse, Recycle, Recreate, Part II:** In-person site visit. newtonconservators.org/property/millennium-park

60. **Utopian Dream:** In-person site visit. mass.gov/locations/ brook-farm-historic-site; newtonconservators.org/ property/brook-farm

61. **The Clapp's Favorite:** In-person site visit. baringgouldbronzeworks.com/public-works/; dorchesterhistoricalsociety.org

62. **Hopeful Sign:** In-person site visit. corita.org

63. **This Old House, Part I:** In-person site visit. dorchesterhistoricalsociety.org/index.php/properties/ the-james-blake-house

64. **Zoo Relic:** In-person site visit. franklinparkcoalition.org/ longcrouch-woods

65. **Restored Ruins:** In-person site visit. franklinparkcoalition.org/schoolmaster-hill

66. **Scenic View:** In-person site visit. boston.gov/parks/ franklin-park

67. **Go with the Flow:** In-person site visit. mass.gov/service-details/new-charles-river-basin-projects; mass.gov/ files/documents/2016/08/sh/charlesriver2002.pdf; nae.usace.army.mil/Missions/Civil-Works/Flood-Risk-Management/Massachusetts/Charles-River-Dam

68. **Bellringers:** In-person site visit. paulmatisse.com/ charlestown-bell

69. **Hot Potatoes:** In-person site visit. rossmiller.com/ross-miller-portfolio

70. **What's in a Name?:** In-person site visit. nps.gov/bost/ learn/historyculture/bhm.htm

71. **Play the Lottery:** In-person experience. (Yes, I won the lottery!) navy.mil/local/constitution

72. **A Head for Dissent:** In-person visit. ussconstitutionmuseum.org/2015/07/02/off-with-his-head

73. **9/11 Tribute:** In-person site visit. massport.com/logan-airport/about-logan/art-landmarks/911-memorial; wbur.org/morningedition/2016/09/08/logan-memorial

74. **Ships in the Night:** In-person site visit. nantucketlightshiplv-112.org

75. **Room to Grow:** In-person site visit. icaboston.org/ica-watershed

76. **Holy Mother of Mary:** In-person site visit. donorionehome.org/Home/About-Us/Learn-More-About-Don-Orione-Home/About-the-Madonna-Shrine

77. **Moving House:** In-person site visit. longyear.org

78. **A Future King Slept Here:** In-person site visit. ktbf.blogspot.com/2008/12/trail-of-thai-royalty-in-massachusetts.html

79. **Teen Hero:** In-person site visit. brooklinehistory.blogspot.com/2009/12/from-snow-sculptures-to-paris-salon-and.html; wickedlocal.com/article/20091111/news/311119758

80. **Paper Trail:** In-person site visit. papermakinghistory.org

81. **Star Search:** In-person site visit. dextersouthfield.org/about/clay-center/index.cfm

82. **Crazy for Cars:** In-person site visit. larzanderson.org

83. **Fine-Feathered Friends:** In-person site visit. brooklinema.gov/1051/Halls-Pond-Sanctuary

84. **Home Office:** In-person site visit. nps.gov/frla/index.htm

85. **Glove Love:** In-person site visit. harriesheder.com/project/glove-cycle

86. Hunger Game: In-person site visit. craigieonmain.com; timeoutmarket.com/boston/eat-and-drink/craigie-burger/; bonappetit.com/people/chefs/article/our-sept-cover

87. Sweet Dreams: In-person site visit. spanglercandy.com/our-brands/necco-wafers

88. Urban Oasis: In-person site visit. kendallcenter.com/events-public-programs/roof-garden

89. Glad Rags: In-person site visit. garmentdistrict.com

90. This Old House, Part II: In-person site visit. fairbankshouse.org

INDEX